D0534659

YOU'RE A BRAVE MAN, DANIEL!

KAY ARTHUR
JANNA ARNDT

HARVEST HOUSE PUBLISHERS
EUGENE, OREGON

Scripture quotations in this book are taken from the New American Standard Bible ®, © 1960, 1962, 1963, 1968, 1971, 1972, 1973, 1975, 1977, 1995 by The Lockman Foundation. Used by permission. (*www.Lockman.org*)

DISCOVER 4 YOURSELF is a registered trademark of The Hawkins Children's LLC. Harvest House Publishers, Inc., is the exclusive licensee of the federally registered trademark DISCOVER 4 YOURSELF.

Illustrations © Steve Bjorkman

Cover by Left Coast Design, Portland, Oregon

YOU'RE A BRAVE MAN, DANIEL!
Copyright © 2007 by Precept Ministries International
Published by Harvest House Publishers
Eugene, Oregon 97402
www.harvesthousepublishers.com

ISBN 978-0-7369-0147-5 (pbk.)
ISBN 978-0-7369-3691-0 (eBook)

All rights reserved. No part of this publication may be reproduced, stored in a retrieval system, or transmitted in any form or by any means—electronic, mechanical, digital, photocopy, recording, or any other—except for brief quotations in printed reviews, without the prior permission of the publisher.

Printed in the United States of America

15   16   17   18   19 / ML-SK /   11   10   9   8   7   6   5

CONTENTS

Studying God's Script—
A Bible Study You Can Do!

STUDYING GOD'S SCRIPT— A BIBLE STUDY YOU CAN DO!

Hey, guys! It's great to have you back on another great Bible adventure. We are on our way (Molly, Sam the great detective beagle, and me) to meet my Aunt Sherry in Hollywood, California. My name is Max. We are going to help out on the set of a brand-new television series that is being made on the Book of Daniel. Daniel is a very interesting, historical book in the Bible that shows us not only WHAT happened in the past, but also WHAT is going to happen in the future. Doesn't that sound *exciting?*

We are going to use God's script, the Bible, to find out WHO the main characters are in the Book of Daniel and WHAT happens to them as God's story unfolds. HOW do Daniel and his friends handle difficult situations? WHAT lessons can we learn about trusting God when bad things happen to us? WHO has visions and dreams? WHAT do these dreams mean? And WHO is in control of all Daniel's circumstances?

This is going to be one *awesome* television series with some unbelievable special effects to capture these special dreams and events! You can take part in creating this exciting series by studying God's Word, the Bible, the source of all truth, and by asking God's Spirit to lead and guide you. You also have this book, which is an inductive Bible study. That word *inductive* means you go straight to the Bible *yourself* to investigate what the Book of Daniel shows us about God and His plan for the future and a young man who is serious about God. In inductive Bible study you discover for yourself what the Bible says and means.

Doesn't that sound like fun? Grab your script on Daniel as we take a look into the past so we can film this action-packed adventure that will take us into the future!

THINGS YOU'LL NEED

New American Standard Bible (Updated Edition)— preferably the New Inductive Study Bible (NISB)

Pen or Pencil   A Dictionary

Colored Pencils   This Workbook

Index Cards

1

WELCOME TO BABYLON... OR MODERN-DAY IRAQ

DANIEL 1

It's great to have you here in sunny California! Molly and I are soooo excited about this new Bible adventure where we'll get to help on a brand-new television series. Miss Leslie, the producer of this series, is a friend of my Aunt Sherry, who developed the comic book on the life of Joseph called *Joseph— God's Superhero*.

Miss Leslie asked Aunt Sherry to come out to California to help her create and direct this fantastic television series on the life of Daniel. Aren't you excited? Not only do we get to learn all about Daniel and how to be like him, but we also get to learn how to create and shoot a television series. Are you ready to get started? Great! Then let's head over to the set and start reading God's script.

DAY ONE

SCAN THE SCRIPT!

"Hey, guys, I see you made it!" Aunt Sherry said with a smile as we walked on the set. "Are you ready to start studying God's script, the Bible?"

"We sure are!" Max replied as he gave Aunt Sherry a hug.

"Great. Then grab your scripts and have a seat in those chairs."

"Look, Max," Molly exclaimed, "our chairs have our names on the back just like in the movies."

"That is so cool!" Max said with a smile. "Look, Sam! Aunt Sherry even has a chair just for you." Sam jumped up into his chair and sat on his haunches looking like Mr. Hollywood. Aunt Sherry, Max, and Molly cracked up laughing. "Okay, WHAT is the first thing you need to do before you open your script?" asked Aunt Sherry.

"Pray," Molly answered. "I'll pray and then we can get started reading our script."

Remember, Bible study should always begin with prayer. We need to ask God to help us understand what the Bible says and to direct us by His Holy Spirit, so we can make sure we understand His Word and handle it accurately.

All right! Now that we have prayed, did you know that Daniel is a book in the Bible that is both historical and prophetic? Since you study history in school, you know that history is about people and events. Prophecy is when God reveals to us what is going to happen in the future. Season One (*You're a Brave Man, Daniel!*) of our new television series will focus on the historical events in Daniel 1–6, while Season Two

(Fast-Forward to the Future) on Daniel 7–12 will show us what is going to happen in the future. Pretty cool, huh?

Now that you know what our television series is going to be about, let's scan our script to make sure we have just the right location to begin taping our television series. Your script is the Observation Worksheets located at the back of this book. These pages have the Bible text printed out for you to use.

Turn to page 134. Read Daniel 1:1-2. To discover the setting and characters for our new television series, we need to ask the 5 W's and an H. WHAT are the 5 W's and an H? They are the WHO, WHAT, WHERE, WHEN, WHY, and HOW questions.

1. Since this book is both a historical and prophetic book, asking WHO is very important. Asking WHO helps you find out:

   WHO are the main characters?

   WHO is this prophecy about?

   WHO is involved?

2. WHAT helps you understand:

   WHAT are the main events taking place?

   WHAT is God telling you?

3. In any historical event, WHERE is very important. And in prophecy it is also important to know WHERE it happens.

   WHERE helps you learn:

   WHERE did something happen?

   WHERE did they go?

   WHERE was this said?

   When we discover a WHERE, we double-underline the WHERE in green.

4. WHEN tells us about time. We mark it with a green clock ⏰ or a green circle like this: ○.

WHEN tells us:

WHEN did this event happen or WHEN is it going to happen?

WHEN is so very important in history and prophecy. It helps us follow the order of events.

5. Looking at history, WHY asks questions like:

WHY did this event happen?

Looking at prophecy, WHY asks:

WHY is God telling us this is going to happen?

6. HOW lets you figure out things like:

HOW did something happen?

HOW did the people react to what happens?

HOW is something going to happen in the future?

HOW does it come to pass?

Now read your script and ask those 5 W's and an H.

Daniel 1:1 WHEN does this scene take place? Draw a green clock or green circle over this time phrase in Daniel 1:1 on page 134. Then circle the correct answer below.

a. the first year of the reign of Jehoiakim

b. the third year of the reign of Jehoiakim

c. the sixth year of the reign of Jehoiakim

WHO are two of the characters in our script?

_____, king of _____ and

_____, king of _____

Look at the chart "The Rulers and Prophets of Daniel's Time," and circle the names of these two rulers.

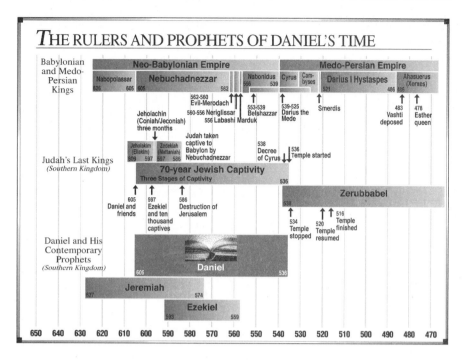

THE RULERS AND PROPHETS OF DANIEL'S TIME

So WHERE are our two kings from?

Daniel 1:1 WHAT is the location of Jehoiakim, the king of Judah? WHERE does Nebuchadnezzar come to?

J __ __ __ __ __ __ __ m

Daniel 1:1-2 WHERE is King Nebuchadnezzar from?

King of B __ __ __ __ __ n, the land of _____

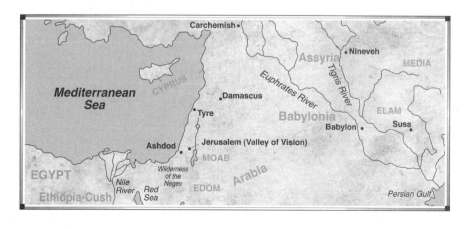

To learn more about the special location King Nebuchadnezzar is from, take a look at the notes of Miss Anna, the production manager, below.

PRODUCTION MANAGER'S NOTES

BABYLON means "gate of God" and is one of the most important cities in the ancient world.

Babylon is located east of the Euphrates River, 56 miles south of present-day Baghdad in Iraq. It is in the fertile plain of Mesopotamia between two rivers: the Tigris and the Euphrates. It lies near the Garden of Eden, near the cradle of civilization.

The first mention of this ancient city in the land of Shinar is found in Genesis 10–11. In Genesis 11, the people of Babel (Babylon) sin by wanting to make a name for themselves instead of having God rule over them. From the beginning of time, this city has been in opposition to God.

Keep your eyes and ears open because Babylon not only plays an important part in history, but it will also play a part in the future. You can study more about Babylon and what happens to it in the future by studying the Book of Revelation in Max and Molly's Bible adventure A SNEAK PEEK INTO THE FUTURE.

Daniel 1:1 WHAT did Nebuchadnezzar come to Jerusalem to do?

_____

Daniel 1:2 WHO wins this battle?

_____

Daniel 1:2 WHO gave King Jehoiakim, the king of Judah, into King Nebuchadnezzar's hand? WHO was in control?

_____

Wow! Are you surprised to see that God gave Jehoiakim into King Nebuchadnezzar's hand? WHY would God allow His chosen people, the sons of Israel, to be taken captive by their enemies? One way we can find out is by looking at some other passages of Scripture. This is called *cross-referencing.*

Look up and read Deuteronomy 28:1-7.

Deuteronomy 28:1 WHAT did the children of Israel need to do to be set high above all the nations of the earth?

"_____ the LORD your God, being careful to _____ all His _____."

Deuteronomy 28:7 WHAT would happen to Israel's enemies if Israel obeyed?

Israel's enemies will be _____.

Read Deuteronomy 28:15,25.

Deuteronomy 28:25 WHAT would happen if Israel did not obey? WHAT would the Lord cause the children of Israel to be?

_____ before your _____

Wow! Look at HOW important it was to God that the children of Israel obey Him! They would defeat their enemies if they obeyed, but if they disobeyed, then they would be defeated.

HOW about you? Do you think God expects you to obey Him?

_____

WHY? _____

HOW are you going to know what God wants you to do? Would studying the Bible help you to know what God expects? HOW would studying the Bible help you?

_____

HOW much do you obey God? Circle one of the answers below.

   a. all the time   b. a lot of the time

   c. sometimes   d. not very often

WHICH answer should you circle? Write it out below:

_____

Now that you have thought about what you do and what you should do, why don't you go to God and ask Him to help you change anything that you need to change, to help you obey Him?

Way to go! You have done some awesome research today. You went straight to God's book, the book of truth. You saw that there are two kings: the king of Judah who is king over God's chosen people, and the king of Babylon, king over a very wicked city who defeats the king of Judah and takes some of the sons of Israel into captivity.

You also saw by looking at other passages of Scripture that God told His people as long as they obeyed Him, they would defeat their enemies. Does that mean the sons of Israel didn't obey God and His commandments since King Nebuchadnezzar takes God's chosen people into captivity? You'll find out tomorrow as you continue the research for our new television series. But before you leave the set today, you need to discover your memory verse for this week.

Did you know that the original language the Bible was written in was Hebrew with some Aramaic in the Old Testament, and Koine Greek in the New Testament? Since the Book of Daniel is written in both the Hebrew and Aramaic languages, we thought it would be fun if you discovered this week's verse by using a fun made-up language that kids like to use called "Pig Latin."

There are different ways to write Pig Latin depending on if a word begins with one consonant, multiple consonants, or a vowel. If a word begins with a single consonant, you take the consonant off the front of the word and put it at the end of the word, adding *ay* after it (such as, if I wanted to say *Daniel* in Pig Latin, I would say *anielday*).

Now if a word begins with two or more consonants, you would take the group of consonants off the front of the word and add them to the end, and then add *ay* to the end of the word. For an example, the word *choice* would become *oicechay*. And if a word starts with a vowel, you just add *ay* to the end of the word. For example, the word *up* would become *upay*.

Solve this week's verse by looking at the words on the next page that are in Pig Latin and writing the real word for this fun made-up language underneath each blank. Then find the reference for your verse in Daniel 1. Practice this verse by saying it in both Pig Latin and English three times in a row, three times today!

utbay   anielDay   ademay   upay   ishay   indmay
____   _____   _____   ____   ____   _____

atthay   ehay   ouldway   otnay   efileday   imselfhay
____   ____   _____   _____   _____   _____

ithway   ethay   ingskay   oicechay   oodfay   oray
_____   _____   _____   _____   _____   ___

ithway   ethay   ineway   ichwhay   ehay   ankdray;
_____   _____   _____   _____   ____   _____;

osay   ehay   oughtsay   ermissionpay   omfray   ethay
____   ____   _____   _____   _____   ____

ommandercay   ofay   ethay   officialsay   atthay   ehay
_____   ____   _____   _____   _____   ____

ightmay   otnay   efileday   imselfhsay.
_____   ____   _____   _____

Daniel 1: _____

You did it! We are so proud of you!

ON THE SET OF ISRAEL

"Look at that, Molly! Isn't that set amazing?" Max asked as they walked onto the set with Aunt Sherry. "It looks just like the pictures I have seen of ancient Jerusalem."

Aunt Sherry told the kids, "This is the set where we will shoot our opening scene as King Nebuchadnezzar comes up against King Jehoiakim to besiege the city."

"Will we start filming today?" Max asked Aunt Sherry.

"Not yet. We need to finish casting our characters. But first you and Molly need to find out WHAT the sons of Israel did that caused God to let them be taken into captivity. After you do your research, you can help me, Miss Leslie, and Mr. Preston, the casting director, finish casting."

"All right!" Molly exclaimed. "Let's get started."

Don't forget to pray! Let's find out WHAT the children of Israel did that caused God to allow them to be defeated. Start by looking at the production manager's notes on the nation of Israel.

PRODUCTION MANAGER'S NOTES

The beginning of the nation of Israel is found in the Book of Genesis as God promises to make Abram (Abraham) a great nation in Genesis 12. This nation is to come through his son, Isaac (Genesis 17:19; Genesis 21:12), and through Isaac's son Jacob (Genesis 28).

In Genesis 35:10, God changes Jacob's name to Israel. Jacob (Israel) has 12 sons, whose descendants are known as the 12 tribes of Israel, God's chosen people.

In 1 Kings, because of King Solomon's divided heart, God divides the 12 tribes of Israel into two kingdoms: the north and the south.

The northern kingdom of Israel is made up of 10 tribes of Israel. They settle in the north and claim Samaria as their capital.

The southern kingdom of Judah is made up of the remaining two tribes of Israel, Benjamin and Judah, who keep Jerusalem as their capital.

So which kingdom has King Nebuchadnezzar come after?

a. the northern kingdom of Israel whose capital is Samaria

b. the southern kingdom of Judah whose capital is Jerusalem

Look at Daniel 1:1 to see if you got the right answer. Let's solve the crossword puzzle below to find out what happens to both of these kingdoms. We need to see if either kingdom does what God tells them to do.

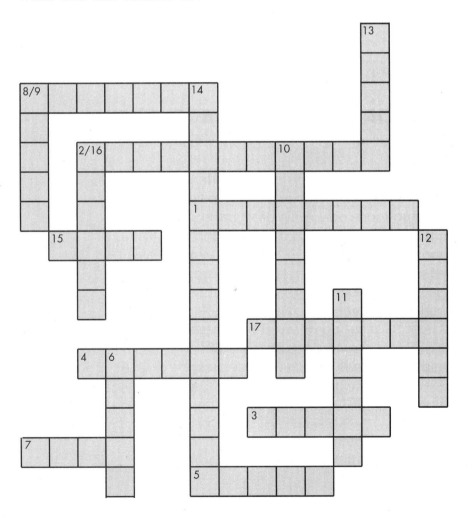

First let's find out what happens to the northern kingdom of Israel. Look up and read 2 Kings 17:5-7,12.

2 Kings 17:6 WHAT did the king of Assyria do?

1. (Across) He _____ Samaria and carried

2. (Down) _____ away into

3. (Across) _____ to Assyria.

WHY did this happen?

2 Kings 17:7 Because the sons of Israel had

4. (Across) _____ against the Lord their God.

2 Kings 17:9 The sons of Israel did things secretly which were not

5. (Across) _____ against the Lord their God.

2 Kings 17:12 They served

6. (Down) _____ .

Now let's complete our puzzle by looking at the southern kingdom of Judah that King Nebuchadnezzar has come after. Look up and read 2 Chronicles 36:5-7.

2 Chronicles 36:5 WHAT did King Jehoiakim do?

7. (Across) He did _____ in the sight of the Lord his God.

2 Chronicles 36:6 WHAT happened when King Nebuchadnezzar came up against King Jehoiakim?

King Nebuchadnezzar

8. (Down) _____ him with bronze chains to take him to

9. (Across) _____ .

2 Chronicles 36:7 WHAT else did King Nebuchadnezzar bring to Babylon?

10. (Down) Some of the _____ of the house of the Lord

WHERE did he put these articles of God?

11. (Down) In his _____ at Babylon

Look up and read Jeremiah 25:8-11.

Jeremiah 25:8 WHAT did the Lord of hosts tell them?

"You have not

12. (Down) _____

13. (Down) My _____."

Jeremiah 25:9 WHAT is the Lord going to do?

14. (Down) "I will send to _____ king of Babylon, My servant, and bring them against this

15. (Across) _____ and against its

16. (Across) _____."

Jeremiah 25:11 HOW long will they be in captivity and serve the king of Babylon?

17. (Across) _____ years

Can you believe it? Both of these kingdoms disobey God and are taken into captivity. The northern kingdom of Israel is taken into captivity by Assyria in 772 BC. Then the southern kingdom of Judah is taken into captivity by the Babylonians in three different sieges of Jerusalem, which begin in 605 BC with King Jehoiakim. Looking at both of these kingdoms, does God do exactly what He says He will do?

Yes! God always does what He says He will do. God told the nation of Israel in Deuteronomy 28 that if they obeyed God, being careful to do all His commandments, they would be set high above all the nations of the earth and their enemies would be defeated. But as we have seen today, they didn't obey. They didn't listen to God. Instead they chose to do things God said were not right. They chose to serve idols instead of worshiping God. They sinned against God. James 4:17 says, *"Therefore, to one who knows the right thing to do and does not do it, to him it is sin."*

That's why we're studying God's Word—so that we can know and do what God says is right. HOW can we apply WHAT we learned about these two kingdoms to our lives? Let's look at how you spend your time.

> WHAT are some of the things that you do every week? Do you play sports, talk with friends on the Internet, or play a musical instrument? Name some of the things you do:
>
> _____
>
> _____
>
> Do you talk to God during the day? Do you have time to study your Bible? Do you let God talk to you through the Bible about His commandments?
>
> _____
>
> _____
>
> Israel got into trouble for worshiping idols. Idols are not just statues. Idols are anything in your life that you put *before* God, like watching television, playing sports, or playing video games. WHAT are some of the things that you put before God?
>
> _____
>
> _____

These activities and things we listed aren't wrong unless you put them in God's place. That's why we want you to check yourself to see how you're spending your time. If God is God, then He should be number one in your life!

Way to go! We are so proud of you for studying and apply-
ing God's Word! Now don't forget to practice your memory
verse. This verse shows you something very important about
our main character's character. Tomorrow we will find out
what happens after King Nebuchadnezzar captures the city.

Day Three

casting call

It's great to have you back on the set! Now that you have
the historical background information for our television series,
are you ready to help Aunt Sherry, Miss Leslie, and Mr. Preston
finish casting our characters? Great! Also, Mr. Andy, the prop
master, needs some help gathering the props for our first scene.
Grab your script (page 134) and let's head back to Daniel 1.
Don't forget to talk to God!

Read Daniel 1:1-7 and ask those 5 W's and an H.

Daniel 1:2 WHEN Jerusalem is besieged,
WHAT is taken from the house of God?
WHAT props do we need?

_____

WHERE are these vessels taken?

_____

Think about how God would feel about His holy
vessels being taken from His house into the house of a
false god. Does King Nebuchadnezzar have respect for
God's holy vessels? _____

Even though it looks like Nebuchadnezzar and his gods are

more powerful since he has taken the city and the holy vessels, WHO did we see was in control in Daniel 1:2? _____

Remember: Even when things look bad, God is still in control.

Now that we have our props, let's cast our characters.

Daniel 1:3 WHOM did King Nebuchadnezzar order the chief of his officials, Ashpenaz, to bring in?

Some of the _____ of _____

Daniel 1:3 WHOM did some of these include?

Some of the _____ _____ and of the _____

Daniel 1:4 Describe these sons of Israel.

They were "y _ _ _ _ s…who were _____-_____, showing _____, endowed with _____ and discerning _____."

Daniel 1:4 WHAT did the king order Ashpenaz to teach them?

_____

Daniel 1:5 WHAT did the king appoint them a daily ration of?

_____

Daniel 1:5 HOW long were they to be educated?

_____

WHAT was to happen to them after they were educated?

_____

Did you notice that each one of these youths (teenagers) who are taken into captivity are considered the best of the best? They are smart, athletic, handsome, the finest in the land of Israel. They are taken from their homes, their language, and their beliefs and put in the king's royal school to be taught the king's language and beliefs.

Daniel 1:6 WHO are the four main characters taken from the sons of Judah?

_____, _____, _____, and

_____

Daniel 1:7 WHAT did the commander of the officials assign to these sons of Israel?

_____

Write out each one of the new names next to their original name.

Daniel: _____   Hananiah: _____

Mishael: _____   Azariah: _____

WHY were these four teenagers given new names? Did you know that in Bible times a person's name was very important because it showed the person's character and identity? Let's look at the meaning of these four guys' Hebrew names. *Daniel* means

"God is my judge," *Hananiah* means "Jehovah has been gracious" (Jehovah and Yahweh are Hebrew names for God), *Mishael* means "Who is what God is" (in other words, there is nobody like God), and *Azariah* means "Yahweh has helped." In each one of these boy's Hebrew names, we see the name of God.

Now look at the meaning of their new Babylonian names. *Belteshazzar* means "Bel will protect," *Shadrach* means "inspired of Aku," *Meshach* means "belonging to Aku," and *Abed-nego* means "servant of Nego." Each one of these Babylonian names has a reference to a false god. Bel, Nego, and Aku were all names of the false gods of the Babylonians.

> Since names showed a person's character and identity, do you think that King Nebuchadnezzar changed these youths' names to change their identity, to show his ownership over them now that they have been taken into captivity? _____

Daniel was about 15 years old when he was taken from his home into captivity. Can you imagine not only being taken from your home, but also being taken to a foreign city, a new school, having your name changed, and not even understanding the language?

> HOW would you feel? Would you be scared, anxious, or confused? Would you think God didn't love you, had forgotten you, or couldn't protect you? Would you continue to trust and follow God in spite of what had happened to you? Write out HOW you would feel and WHAT you would do.

_____

_____

_____

HOW would it feel to have the people who captured you brag that their god was stronger than your God, especially since you know it's not true?

HOW will Daniel and his friends handle being taken to a foreign country of a heathen king who doesn't know God and respect His holy vessels? Any hopes and dreams they had for their future have just been shattered. They are no longer free; they will never return home to see their families again. Will they become angry over their circumstances? Will they bend under the pressure? Will they change what they believe, or will they continue to love and trust God in spite of everything that has happened to them? We'll find out. You have done an awesome job at casting our characters! Don't forget to practice your memory verse.

CAMERA CHECK

"Hey, Max, why don't you and Molly come help me get these props ready for our camera check?" Mr. Andy asked as Max and Molly arrived on the set of Babylon.

"Sure, Mr. Andy. We'd love to help," Max said. "Oh man, these props are making me hungry. Look at all these great things to eat." Molly laughed. "So, Max, which would you rather have: the king's choice food or these yummy vegetables?"

Before Max could answer, Aunt Sherry walked onto the set. "The king's table looks great. Are you ready for us to do our camera check, Andy?"

"I think we're ready," replied Andy.

How about you? Let's grab our scripts and make sure Mr. Andy has all the props for our next scene. Pray and then turn to page 135. Read Daniel 1:8-21. Ask the 5 W's and an H to prepare for our camera check.

Daniel 1:8 WHAT did Daniel do?

Daniel _____ _____ his m__ __ __.

Do you know what it means to make up your mind? Making up your mind is making a decision in your heart. It's like drawing a line in the sand and saying, "This is what I believe. This is what I will do. I will not cross over this line."

Daniel 1:8 WHAT did Daniel make up his mind about?

_____

Daniel 1:8 WHAT did Daniel seek?

He sought _____ from the _____ of the _____ that he might not _____ himself.

To defile means to make unclean, dirty, or corrupt. WHY would eating the king's choice food and wine corrupt or make Daniel unclean? Did you know that God chose the nation of Israel to be a holy people set apart from all the other peoples on the face of the earth?

God gives the sons of Israel laws for their food that show

them what is clean and okay to eat, and what is unclean and not okay to eat. If you want to read about these laws, you can find them in Leviticus 11 and Deuteronomy 14. Daniel knows God's law and chooses to honor God by what he eats and drinks.

Daniel 1:9 WHAT does God grant Daniel?

_____

Daniel 1:10 WHY was the commander of the officials afraid to change Daniel's food and drink?

_____

Daniel 1:11-12 WHAT did Daniel ask the overseer to do?

"To _____ your servants for _____ days"

Daniel 1:12 WHAT did Daniel ask for them to be given to eat and drink?

_____

Daniel 1:15 WHAT happened after they were tested for 10 days?

_____

_____

Daniel 1:11-17 WHO took the test—all of the youths or just four of the youths (Daniel and his three friends)? Circle the correct answer.

a. All of the youths

b. Four of the youths: Daniel, Hananiah, Mishael, and Azariah

Daniel 1:17 WHAT did God give these four youths?

_____ and _____ in every branch of _____ and _____

Daniel 1:17 WHAT did Daniel understand?

_____

Daniel 1:18-20 WHAT happened to them when they were presented before Nebuchadnezzar?

Not _____ was found like _____, _____, _____, and _____; so they entered the _____ _____ _____.

HOW did these guys get to be so smart? Look back at Daniel 1:17 if you missed it.

_____

Daniel 1:21 HOW long did Daniel continue?

_____

Wow! Daniel and his friends are teenagers far away from home in a wicked city, where no one will ever know if they give in to temptation and follow the crowd. But instead of giving in when they are tested, they do what God says is right.

HOW about you? WHAT would you do if you knew no one would find out? Would you lie to your parents about where you are going and whom you are going to be with? Would you drink, smoke, inhale something to make you feel different, or take drugs? Or would you dare to go against the crowd and do what God says is right? Write out what you would do:

_____
_____
_____

Look at how God honored these four teenagers' decision to do what He says is right. Their appearances were better than the other youths, and God gave them knowledge, intelligence, and wisdom. They each entered into the king's personal service. Pretty cool, huh?

All right! Our camera check is finished and we are ready to start filming. Tomorrow we will get a close-up of God and one of our awesome teenagers.

ZOOMING IN

"All right, quiet on the set. We are ready to roll," Aunt Sherry called out. "Camera One, I want you to zoom in right after the opening sequence. Let's count it down, and…action."

Are you ready to "zoom in" and take a closer look at God and Daniel? Great! Don't forget to ask God for His help. Pull out your script and let's get a close-up on both God and Daniel.

One way you can uncover clues about the main events and characters in the Book of Daniel is to mark them in a special way so you can get a closer look at them. Today we are going to "zoom in" on our scripts and mark every place we see *God* and *Daniel*. We also need to mark each pronoun that refers to either God or Daniel. WHAT are pronouns? Check out Max and Molly's notes below.

Pronouns

Pronouns are words that take the place of nouns. A noun is a person, place, or thing. A pronoun stands in for a noun! Here's an example: "Molly and Max are excited about helping on the new television series on Daniel. They can't wait to discover what happens to Daniel now that he has been taken into captivity." The word *they* is a pronoun because it takes the place of Molly and Max's names in the second sentence. It is another word we use to refer to Molly and Max.

Watch for these other pronouns when you are marking people's names:

I	you	he	she
me	yours	him	her
mine		his	hers
we	it		
our	its		
they	them		

Now that you know what pronouns are, turn to your Observation Worksheets on page 134. Read Daniel 1 and mark *God* and *Daniel* in a special way, just like we have listed below:

God (draw a purple triangle and color it yellow)

Daniel (color it blue)

All right! Now look in your script at each verse where you marked *God* in Daniel 1:2, 9, and 17. Let's find out what you learned about God from each of these verses. We want to make sure our television viewers know the truth about WHO God is and WHAT He does, so that they can get to know Him, too! Make a list of everything you learned about God in the box below.

WHAT I Learned About God

Daniel 1:2

Daniel 1:9

Daniel 1:17

Amazing! Stop and think about WHAT this list shows us about WHO God is, about His power, and about WHAT He can do.

In Daniel 1:2, the Lord gave the outcome of the battle. God is the One who allowed Jerusalem to be defeated by King Nebuchadnezzar and allowed Daniel and the other youths to be taken into captivity. God is the One in control of people. This shows us that God is sovereign. There is absolutely nothing that God doesn't have control over!

In Daniel 1:9, God is the One who got other people to show favor and compassion to Daniel. God loves us! He cares about what happens to us.

In Daniel 1:17, God gave the four youths knowledge, intelligence, and wisdom. What an *awesome* God! Would God do this for you?

Let's make a list on WHAT we know about Daniel by looking at where we marked his name on our script. Put the facts in the box below.

WHAT I Learned About Daniel

Wow! Would you like to be like Daniel? Let's do a character profile on Daniel to see if you could play Daniel's part.

CHARACTER PROFILE

Daniel	Me

Daniel has faith.

Faith is believing God; it is taking Him at His Word. Faith is when you believe what God says in the Bible, and it shows by the way you act. You decide to do what God says is right. Daniel believes God. He does what God says is right. He chooses to trust God in a very hard and difficult situation.

Do you have faith?

Have you placed your trust in Jesus Christ?

Yes _____   No _____

Do you do what God says is right? Name one thing you do that shows you love and trust God. Here are some examples: Do you read your Bible every day? Do you obey your parents? Do you want to please God? Do you listen and pay attention to His Word? Do you believe God means what He says and act like it? Do you ask God to help you not to lie, steal, gossip, or talk about other kids?

Write out one way that shows you have faith:

_____

_____

Daniel has integrity.

Integrity is doing the right thing when no one is looking. Integrity is being trustworthy and sincere. A person with integrity has the highest standards and is honest, pure, and consistent.

Look at Daniel's integrity. He has the highest standards. Daniel makes up his mind not to defile himself. He keeps himself pure. He sets himself

Do you have integrity?

Can your parents trust you to obey them when they are not around? Have you made up your mind to live God's way, to keep yourself pure? Name a standard that you have set for yourself, like waiting to get married before having sex, or deciding not to drink alcohol.

_____

WHAT would you do if you spent

Daniel

apart from the world he is living in. Daniel dares to be different.

Daniel has courage.

Courage is boldness; it is taking a stand and doing what you know is right even though you are afraid. Daniel took a stand, even though he didn't know what would happen to him if he went against the king's command and refused the food from his table.

Me

the night with friends and they are watching things on TV or looking at things on the Internet that are wrong? Would you go along, or would you say, "This doesn't please God. I can't look at or be a part of this"? Write out what you would do:

_____

_____

WHAT if Mom or Dad were looking over your shoulder while you were on the Internet? Would you slip into code language, or do you have such integrity that Mom and Dad could read what you are writing?

_____

Do you have courage?

Will you be brave like Daniel and stand up for what you know is right, even if it means you will not be cool or popular and that others will laugh at you? Write out one way you will have courage. Write out what you will do when someone tries to get you to do the wrong thing:

_____

_____

_____

_____

Daniel	Me

Daniel

Daniel has humility.

Humility is a lack of pride. Humility is knowing our weaknesses as well as our strengths. Daniel humbled himself before the commander of the officials. He asked for permission not to eat the king's food and wine. He submitted himself to his authority. He was respectful. How about you?

Daniel has self-discipline.

Self-discipline is learning to train and control your behavior. It is being able to turn away from temptation. It is choosing to do right even when it is hard and difficult. It is sticking with something, even though it is dull and boring. It requires determination and sacrifice. How tempting do you think it was for Daniel to look at the king's choice food and not eat it? Daniel disciplined himself. He did not give in to temptation. He chose to do what was right, even though it was hard and difficult.

Me

Are you humble?

Do you submit yourself to those who are in authority over you?

_____Yes _____ No

Are you respectful? HOW do you treat your parents and your teachers?

_____

HOW do you talk about them to your friends when they aren't around to hear you?

_____

Do you have self-discipline?

WHAT do you eat? Do you choose healthy foods or junk foods?

_____

Training yourself to eat healthy foods, playing sports or a musical instrument, memorizing God's Word, saving for something you want to buy, doing your homework, and cleaning your room without being asked are all things that take self-discipline. Name one thing you do that shows you have self-discipline:

_____

_____

What an *awesome* teenager! Look at how Daniel's character is revealed in these hard and difficult circumstances. Daniel dares to be different—he trusts God. Dare to be different. Ask God to help you be a Daniel in your world. Don't follow the crowd to be cool and popular. Make up your mind to honor and live for God!

How do you think Daniel developed such strong character? Could it be because he started learning God's Word when he was younger, like you? That's why we are so proud of you! You are learning to be like Daniel.

Don't forget to say your memory verse out loud to a grown-up this week. Ask the person to tell you something that he or she made up their mind about. Next week we will film a very interesting dream. WHO has this dream, and WHAT does it mean?

2

A KING'S DREAM

DANIEL 2

It's great to have you back on the set. Last week as we began filming our television series, we saw King Nebuchadnezzar besiege Jerusalem, and God allowed the sons of Israel to be taken into captivity. Four awesome teenagers stand out from the rest because they make up their minds to trust God and do what He says is right.

Pretty amazing! Did you make up your mind to be brave like Daniel and do what God says is right? Way to go! WHAT will we discover this week? Let's head back to the set to find out.

DAY ONE

LIGHTS, CAMERA, ACTION...

"That looks so cool," Molly said to Max as they walked on set and she spotted King Nebuchadnezzar's bedroom.

"I bet Aunt Sherry is opening the scene with Nebuchadnezzar dreaming," Max replied.

"You're right, Max." Aunt Sherry smiled as she greeted the kids. "That's exactly how we're opening up. Sam, stop bothering Mr. Hunter. Quit pulling on his pant leg. He's one of our gaffers."

"Cool it, Sam," Max told Sam as he picked him up. "Sorry about that, Mr. Hunter. What does a gaffer do?"

"It's okay, Max. A gaffer works with the lighting. He's an electrician or a lighting technician. Sam just isn't sure about all these lights and wires."

"Are you and Molly ready to get to work on your scripts," Aunt Sherry asked, "while Mr. Hunter makes sure the lighting is just right?"

"We sure are," answered Molly. "I'll pray. Then we can mark our scripts so we'll be ready when the action starts."

Don't forget to talk to God! Now you're going to mark key words on your Observation Worksheets.

What are *key words*? Key words are words that pop up more than once. They are called key words because they help unlock the meaning of the chapter or book that you are studying and give you clues about what is most important in a passage of Scripture.

- Key words are usually used over and over again.
- Key words are important.
- Key words are used by the writer for a reason.

Once you discover a key word, you need to mark it in a special way using a special color or symbol so that you can immediately spot it in Scripture.

Look at the key-word box on the next page. These are the key words for Daniel 2 that you will mark this week. You may also want to make a bookmark for these key words so that you can see them at a glance as you mark them on your Observation Worksheets.

So let's get started. Make your key-word bookmark by taking an index card and writing the key words listed in the box below, as well as how you are going to mark them on your Observation Worksheets.

Then turn to page 136. Read Daniel 2:1-12 and mark your key words in these verses on your Observation Worksheets.

Key Words for Daniel 2

God (draw a purple triangle and color it yellow, or just color it yellow)

Daniel (color it blue)

Nebuchadnezzar (color it orange)

dream (vision) (draw a blue cloud around it)

mystery (box it in orange and color it green)

kingdom (draw a purple crown and color it blue)

Don't forget to mark your pronouns! And mark anything that tells you WHERE by double-underlining the <u>WHERE</u> in green. Mark anything that tells you WHEN by drawing a green clock or green circle like this: ◯ .

Now let's find out what upsets King Nebuchadnezzar and keeps him from sleeping in our opening scene. Ask those 5 W's and an H.

Daniel 2:1 WHEN is this happening? (Did you remember to put a green clock over this time phrase?)

In the _____ year of the reign of _____

Daniel 2:1 WHAT troubles Nebuchadnezzar's spirit and causes him to lose sleep? He has a _____.

Daniel 2:2 WHAT does King Nebuchadnezzar want the magicians, the conjurers, the sorcerers, and the Chaldeans to tell the king?

_____

Daniel 2:4 WHAT language did the Chaldeans speak to the king?

    a. Hebrew   b. Aramaic

Do you remember from Week One that Daniel was written in both the Hebrew and Aramaic languages? Daniel 1 is written in the Hebrew language, which is the language of the sons of Israel (the Jews). Daniel 2–7 is written in Aramaic, which was the language of Nebuchadnezzar and the Gentile nations.

Daniel 2:4 WHAT did the Chaldeans want the king to do?

_____

Daniel 2:5 WHAT would the king do to them if they did not tell both the dream and the interpretation?

_____

Daniel 2:8-9 WHY did the king want them to tell both? WHAT did the king think they would do if he told them the dream?

They would agree together and _____ _____ and _____ _____ until the situation is changed.

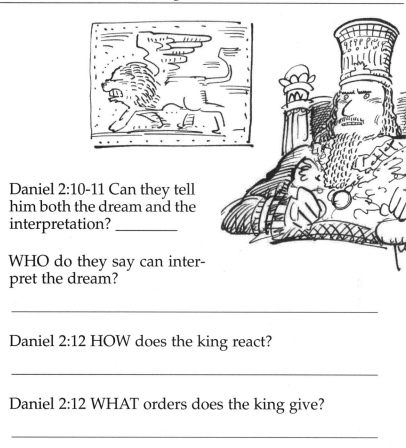

Daniel 2:10-11 Can they tell him both the dream and the interpretation? _____

WHO do they say can interpret the dream?

_____

Daniel 2:12 HOW does the king react?

_____

Daniel 2:12 WHAT orders does the king give?

_____

Wow! Can you believe this? King Nebuchadnezzar is so angry that he gives orders to destroy all the wise men of Babylon. WHOM do these orders include? We'll find out as we continue filming this exciting episode tomorrow!

But before we leave today, we need to discover our new memory verse. Become the script person to make sure Daniel gets his lines just right in our second episode that blesses the God of heaven. Look at the words inside Daniel's thoughts on the next page. As the script person, you need to place each word where it needs to go on our cue card that follows.

Then look up Daniel 2 and find the reference for this verse. Don't forget: You need to learn these lines and practice them three times in a row, three times every day to remind you of WHO God is and how to praise Him for what He has done for you!

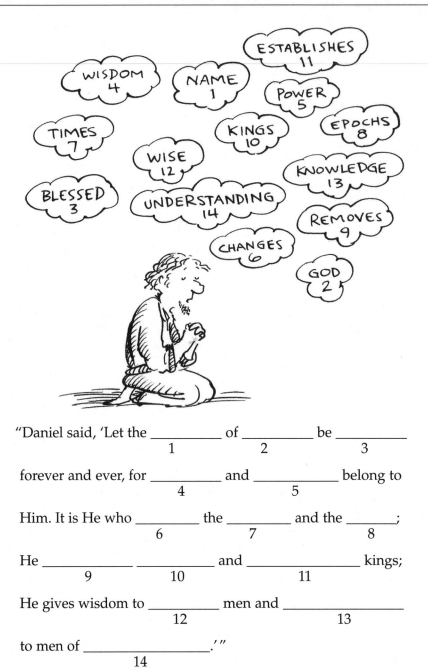

"Daniel said, 'Let the _____ of _____ be _____

forever and ever, for _____ and _____ belong to

Him. It is He who _____ the _____ and the _____;

He _____ _____ and _____ kings;

He gives wisdom to _____ men and _____

to men of _____.' "

Daniel 2: ____-____

Great work! You did it!

SCAN THE SCRIPT!

"Watch out, Mr. Hunter," Max called as he and Molly walked onto the set. "Here comes Sam!"

Mr. Hunter laughed as he caught Sam. "Oh no you don't, boy. I have heard all about your famous face-licking. You come over here and hop up into your chair. Good boy. Ahhh, you got me!"

"Thanks, Mr. Hunter," Max laughed. "He got so excited when he heard your voice that he broke away. He has decided that you're his new friend."

"I'm glad to hear that, except for the face-licking that comes with it. Are you and Molly ready to find out what happens now that King Nebuchadnezzar is furious with all the wise men of Babylon?"

"We sure are," Molly answered.

"Great! Then why don't you pray, and you can get started marking your script while we do a final check on our lighting?"

All right! Now that you have talked to God, turn to page 39 for a list of your key words to mark or use your key-word bookmark.

Start scanning your script. Turn to page 138. Read Daniel 2:13-18 and mark your key words in these verses on your Observation Worksheets.

We are ready to film. Ask those 5 W's and an H and watch the action unfold.

Daniel 2:13 WHO is included in those orders to destroy all the wise men of Babylon? WHO else is going to be killed?

Daniel 2:14 HOW does Daniel reply to the king's bodyguard who comes to kill them?

With _____ and _____

Daniel 2:16 WHAT does Daniel do?

_____

Just look at our awesome young man! Here he is about to be put to death, and yet he has the courage to ask the king to give him time so he can tell him the dream.

Daniel 2:17 WHAT does Daniel do?

_____

Daniel 2:18 WHAT does Daniel ask his friends to do?

_____

WHAT is this that our four young men are doing? They are praying. They are asking God for compassion. To have compassion is to feel someone else's sorrow and suffering, to help them. Daniel and his friends are asking God to help them, to give them the answer to the mystery. Daniel has faith. He has so much confidence in God that he tells the king that he will give the meaning of his dream.

Do you have a faith like Daniel's? _____

WHAT do you do when you are in a crisis? Do you run to God who has all the answers, or do you run to your friends for their answers?

_____

_____

Think about this for a minute. If you run to your friends instead of God, do you think your friends are smarter than God? Can they tell you what is going to happen in the future? Can they control kings? Only God knows the future. He is the only One who has the power to control people and events. Write out what you will do the next time you are scared and in trouble:

_____

_____

What will happen to Daniel and his three friends? Will God answer their prayers? Will the king change his mind about killing all the wise men? Hang in there! We'll find out! Don't forget to practice your memory verse.

SPOTLIGHT ON THE GOD OF HEAVEN

Yesterday was pretty intense as we left Daniel and his three friends requesting compassion from God to solve the mystery and give Daniel the answer to the king's dream. Are you ready to find out what happens? Then grab those scripts and shine the spotlight on the God of heaven. Turn to page 138. Read Daniel 2:19-30 and mark the key words listed on page 39 for these verses on your Observation Worksheets or use your key-word bookmark.

Don't forget to mark your pronouns! And mark anything that tells you WHERE by double-underlining the <u>WHERE</u> in green. Mark anything that tells you WHEN by drawing a green clock 🕐 or green circle like this:◯.

Now be a gaffer and shine God's spotlight. Ask the 5 W's and an H questions.

Daniel 2:19 Does God answer Daniel and his friends'
prayers? WHAT does it say in verse 19?

"The _____ was _____ to _____
in a _____ _____."

Look at Daniel 2:23. WHAT does Daniel say?

"For You have _____ me _____ and
_____; even now You have made _____
to me what we _____ of You, for You have
_____ _____ to us the _____ matter."

Isn't that *awesome!* Daniel and his friends trusted God, and
God gives the answer. When you don't know what to do, when
you need an answer, why don't you do what Daniel did? Ask
God. Seek help from Him. God is the Revealer of mysteries. He
has the answers that you need!

Daniel 2:19-23 WHAT does Daniel do when he receives
his answer?

Daniel _____ the God of heaven.

Aren't these verses wonderful? They tell us so much about
WHO God is! Make a list in the box below of all the things you
learned about God in Daniel 2:19-23.

What I Learned About God

Daniel 2:19

Daniel 2:20

Daniel 2:21

Daniel 2:22

Daniel 2:23

Just look at all you have discovered today! Our second episode in our television series opens with a very upset king who is disturbed over a dream that none of his wise men can interpret. So he decides to kill all the wise men, including Daniel and his three friends who are still in training in King Nebuchadnezzar's school.

HOW do Daniel and his friends handle another scary situation? They run to God and ask for His answer, and God gives it. Wow!

> Daniel 2:24 WHAT does Daniel tell Arioch after he received his answer from God?
>
> "Do not _____ the _____ _____ of Babylon! Take me into the _____ _____, and I will declare the _____."
>
> Daniel 2:25-28 WHO did Daniel tell the king had revealed the mystery of the dream?
>
> _____

What does this show us about Daniel? Daniel is humble. He gives God the glory. He doesn't take the credit for himself.

> Daniel 2:28-29 WHAT is God making known to King Nebuchadnezzar through this dream?
>
> _____

Isn't that amazing! God is going to show this king who doesn't have a relationship with Him what is going to happen in the future! God is a God who reveals the profound and hidden things.

WHAT is this king's dream and WHAT does it mean? We'll find out as we continue to shoot our second episode in this exciting new series.

ZOOMING IN: WHAT'S THE KING'S DREAM?

You did a great job yesterday as you focused the spotlight on God and watched as He answered Daniel's prayer. Today we are ready to shoot a very important scene as we zoom in close to get our first look at King Nebuchadnezzar's dream. Don't forget to pray!

Turn to page 140. Read Daniel 2:31-35 and mark your key words for these verses on your Observation Worksheets using the list on page 39 or your key-word bookmark.

Don't forget to mark your pronouns! And mark anything that tells you WHERE by double-underlining the WHERE in green.

Daniel 2:31 WHAT did King Nebuchadnezzar dream about?

_____

Look at the picture of this awesome statue on page 49. You're going to color this statue just the way King Nebuchadnezzar dreamed it. Don't worry about the lines out to the side that divide the statue. You will find out what to put on those lines tomorrow.

Daniel 2:32 WHAT is the head of the statue made of?

_____

Color the head this color.

WHAT are the breast and arms made of?

_____

Color the arms and the breast.

WHAT are the belly and the thighs made of?

_____

Color the belly and the thighs.

Daniel 2:33 WHAT are the legs made of?

_____

Color the legs.

WHAT are the feet made of? _____ and _____

Color the feet.

Daniel 2:34 WHAT do you learn about the stone?

It was _____ out _____ _____.
It _____ the _____ on its _____ of
iron and clay and _____ them.

Daniel 2:35 WHAT happened after the stone crushed
the feet?

_____

_____

WHAT happened to the stone?

It became a _____ _____ and filled the

_____ _____.

Did you know that mountains in the Bible are sometimes symbols of kingdoms? Pretty amazing! Tomorrow we will find out just what this dream means. Don't forget to praise God by practicing your memory verse. See you on the set!

DAY FIVE

QUIET ON THE SET

Wow! Were you surprised when Daniel revealed the king's dream of an awesome statue? Are you ready to find out what God tells Daniel is going to happen in the future?

Quiet on the set! Let's ask God for His help so we can uncover the meaning of King Nebuchadnezzar's dream. Turn to page 140. Read Daniel 2:36-49 and mark your key words from page 39 on the Observation Worksheets or use your key-word bookmark.

Don't forget to mark the pronouns! And mark anything that tells you WHERE by double-underlining the <u><u>WHERE</u></u> in green. Mark anything that tells you WHEN by drawing a green clock 🕐 or green circle like this: ○ .

Daniel 2:37-38 WHAT did Daniel tell Nebuchadnezzar?

"You, O King, are the _____ ___ _____ to whom the God of heaven has given the _____, the _____, the _____ and the _____... [God] has caused you to _____ over them all. You are the _____ of _____."

Isn't it amazing that God would reveal this to King Nebuchadnezzar? Turn back to the picture of your statue on page 49. On the line beside the head of gold write "Nebuchadnezzar, king of Babylon."

Daniel 2:39 WHAT will there be after King Nebuchadnezzar?

_____ _____ that is _____ to King Nebuchadnezzar's.

Put a number 2 over this kingdom in your script on page 141 and turn back to your statue on page 49. On the line beside the breast and arms of silver, write "After Nebuchadnezzar, inferior kingdom." Right now we don't know who this kingdom is, just that it will be inferior to Nebuchadnezzar's.

Daniel 2:39 WHAT do you learn about the third kingdom?

A kingdom of _____, which will _____ over all the _____.

Put a number 3 over this kingdom in your script and turn

back to your statue on page 49. On the line beside the belly and
thighs of bronze, write "Kingdom will rule over all the earth."

Daniel 2:40-43 WHAT do you learn about the fourth
kingdom?

_____ as i __ __ n, it will _____ and
_____ all these in _____.

It will be a d __ __ __ __ __ d kingdom.

Some of it will be _____ and some of it will be

_____.

Put a number 4 over this kingdom in your script and turn
back to your statue on page 49. On the line beside the legs of
iron, write "Strong kingdom will crush and shatter." And by
the feet of iron and clay, write "Divided kingdom, part strong,
part brittle."

Daniel 2:42-44 WHAT do the toes of the feet represent?
Read these verses again. Verse 42 is talking about the
toes, and in verse 43 it says "they," referring to the toes,
and in verse 44 it says WHAT?

"In the days of those _____." The toes are k __ __ __ s!

HOW many toes does a person have? _____ toes

So HOW many kings will there be? _____ kings

Daniel 2:44 WHAT is going to happen in those days?

The _____ of heaven will set up a _____.

Daniel 2:44-45 WHAT do we learn about God's kingdom?

It will never be _____, it will not be left
for another _____, it will _____ and put
an _____ to all these _____, but it will
endure _____.

Daniel 2:34-35 WHAT part of our picture represents God's kingdom? WHAT did we learn about the stone? WHAT did it do?

It s _ _ _ _ _ the statue on its _____ and c _ _ _ _ _ _ _ the i _ _ _, the _____, the _____, the _____ and the _____ all at the same time.

Turn back to your statue on page 49. On the line beside the stone, write "God's kingdom will never be destroyed. Crushes all of the kingdoms. Endures forever!"

Aren't you excited? You have just discovered something very, very important. You have just found out WHEN Jesus will come back a second time and set up His kingdom on earth. You know from looking at Daniel 2:44 that God's kingdom will be set up in the days of the ten kings ruling on the earth. Has this happened yet? No. You know that Jesus will not return to set up His kingdom until there are ten kings ruling on the earth.

Now let's find out WHAT happens to Daniel after he interprets the meaning of this dream.

Daniel 2:46 WHAT did King Nebuchadnezzar do?

_____

_____

Daniel 2:47 WHAT did Nebuchadnezzar say about Daniel's God?

_____

Daniel 2:48 WHAT happened to Daniel?

_____

_____

_____

Daniel 2:49 WHAT happened to Daniel's friends Shadrach, Meshach, and Abed-nego?

_____

Isn't that fantastic? King Nebuchadnezzar actually bowed before his captive Daniel. Look at how God has taken care of these four awesome young men who put their trust in Him and sought Him for the answers!

Amazing! God has just shown you what is going to happen in the future. You know there will be four kingdoms before Jesus comes back and sets up His kingdom on earth.

Now WHAT is the name of the kingdom that King Nebuchadnezzar is ruling?

_____

HOW many of these kingdoms have already happened today, at our time in history? You'll find out as we continue to study the Book of Daniel. Hang in there! This is a cliff-hanger!

3

A FIERY FURNACE

Wasn't it exciting to watch God answer Daniel's prayer and give a very proud and self-willed king a glimpse into the future? You got a glimpse, too, and discovered that Jesus will not return to set up His kingdom until there are ten kings ruling on the earth. Pretty cool, huh?

Are you ready to find out what happens next? Let's head back to the set and get started on our new episode.

DAY ONE

SCENE ONE: AN IMAGE OF GOLD

"Hey, Mr. Andy, that's an awesome statue! What's it made of?" Max asked as he and Molly looked over Mr. Andy's huge prop for the third episode. Sam ran around in circles barking and growling. "Calm down, Sam," Max laughed, "it's not real. Come on, boy. We need to go help the actors run their lines before Aunt Sherry is ready to film."

Grab those scripts, and don't forget to talk to God! Help the actors run their lines. Turn to page 142. Read Daniel 3:1-6 and mark the key words listed on the next page for these verses on your Observation Worksheets. Then add any new words to your key-word bookmark.

Key-Word List for Daniel 3

God (draw a purple triangle and color it yellow)

Nebuchadnezzar (color it orange)

image (color it yellow)

worship (circle it in purple and color it blue)

deliver (draw a blue ⏝ and color it red)

furnace of blazing fire (seven times more than it was usually heated, midst of the fire) (draw red fire around it)

Don't forget to mark your pronouns! And mark anything that tells you WHERE by double-underlining the <u>WHERE</u> in green. Mark anything that tells you WHEN by drawing a green clock ⏰ or green circle like this: ◯.

Great work! Our scripts are marked and our actors are ready to go. Let's ask the 5 W's and an H so we can help Mr. Andy get set up for this opening scene.

Daniel 3:1 WHAT prop do we need? WHAT did King Nebuchadnezzar make?

_____

_____

HOW big was this image of gold (the statue)?

_____

_____

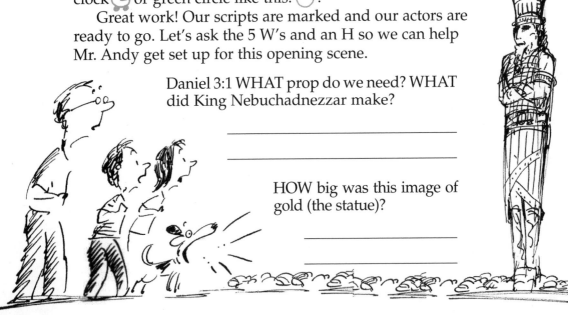

In our measurements, this would make the statue (the image of gold) 90 feet tall and 9 feet wide. Can you imagine a statue that tall? Why do you think that King Nebuchadnezzar built this huge image of gold? Could it be because of his dream?

A lot of Bible scholars believe that Nebuchadnezzar built this statue (the image of gold) in direct defiance of God. Remember, his dream meant that his great kingdom would end. He was only the head of gold, and there were three other kingdoms that would come after his. It's like he was saying to God, "Oh no, my kingdom isn't going to end! It's going to last forever!" King Nebuchadnezzar makes a mistake in thinking that he can change what's going to happen in the future, that he can change God's Word.

Daniel 3:1 WHERE is our setting? WHERE did King Nebuchadnezzar set up this image of gold?

Look at the map below. Find Babylon on your map. The city of Dura isn't shown on this map, but it would be about six miles south of Babylon.

NORTH

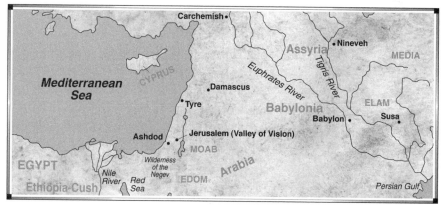

SOUTH

Daniel 3:2 To WHAT did King Nebuchadnezzar send word for all the satraps, prefects, governors, counselors, treasurers, judges, magistrates, and all the rulers of the provinces to come?

The _____ of the _____

Daniel 3:3-5 WHAT command was given to the people when they heard the music begin?

They were to _____ _____ and _____ the golden _____ that Nebuchadnezzar had set up.

Daniel 3:6 WHAT would happen if they didn't fall down and worship the image?

_____

Why don't you fast-forward to the future just for a minute by looking up and reading Revelation 13:14-17 in your Bible.

Revelation 13:14 TO WHOM was there to be an image?

_____

Revelation 13:15 WHAT would happen to those who did not worship the image of the beast?

_____

Can you believe that one day in the future there will be another image that those who dwell on the earth will have to worship or be killed? You can learn more about this beast, his image, and the future in Max and Molly's Revelation adventure, *A Sneak Peek into the Future.*

WHAT will happen on the plain of Dura? Will anyone refuse to bow down and worship Nebuchadnezzar's image of gold? We'll find out. But before we head out today, let's discover our new memory verse.

Look at the sound engineer's mixing board below. To discover this week's verse, look at the words written on the sound engineer's board. Put an X through each word on the board if it is a sound.

After you have crossed out all the sounds, take the words that are left on the board, starting with the words in the left handed column and then working through each column and placing them in order on the blanks underneath. Don't forget to find the reference for this verse in Daniel, chapter 3.

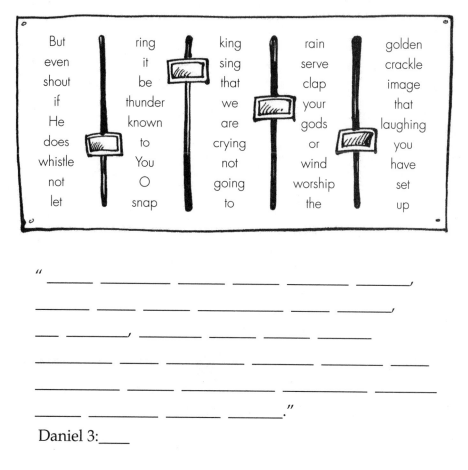

" _____ _____ _____ _____ _____ _____,

_____ _____ _____ _____ _____ _____,

___ _____, _____ _____ _____ _____ _____

_____ _____ _____ _____ _____ _____

_____ _____ _____ _____ _____ _____

_____ _____ _____ _____."

Daniel 3:____

All right! Now practice saying your memory verse three times in a row, three times today!

SCENE TWO: SOUND THE MUSIC

Hey, guys, welcome back to the set. Are you ready to find out what happens when the music sounds on the plain of Dura? All right! Why don't you help Mr. Morgan, the sound engineer? A sound engineer manages an audio crew that handles all the sounds on a television show. He or she uses monitors to help see what the camera sees, and a mixing board to balance all the sounds. A sound engineer needs to be fast-thinking and able to adapt to anything.

First talk to God. Then mark your script so that you will be ready to help Mr. Morgan. Be part of the audio crew and cue the musicians. Turn to page 143. Read Daniel 3:7-13 and mark the key words listed on page 56 for these verses on your Observation Worksheets or use your key-word bookmark.

Don't forget to mark the pronouns! And mark anything that tells you WHERE by double-underlining the WHERE in green. Mark anything that tells you WHEN by drawing a green clock or green circle like this: ○ .

Now watch those monitors. Ask the 5 W's and an H.

Daniel 3:7 WHO bowed down and worshiped the image when the sound of the horn, flute, lyre, trigon, psaltery, bagpipe, and all kinds of music were heard?

All the _____, _____ and _____ of every _____

Daniel 3:8 WHAT did certain Chaldeans come forward to do?

_____

Daniel 3:10 WHAT was the decree they reminded King Nebuchadnezzar of?

_____

Daniel 3:11 WHAT would happen if they didn't fall down and worship?

_____

Daniel 3:12 WHAT did the Chaldeans tell King Nebuchadnezzar about Shadrach, Meshach, and Abed-nego?

_____

_____

Daniel 3:13 HOW did Nebuchadnezzar react? WHAT emotion does he show in this scene?

_____

Daniel 3:13 WHAT orders does King Nebuchadnezzar give?

_____

Wow! Three of our awesome teenagers are in trouble. They have not bowed to worship the image, and some of the Chaldeans just can't wait to tell the king that the Jews he has appointed over the province of Babylon have disregarded his command.

WHY didn't Shadrach, Meshach, and Abed-nego bow down and worship this image? Just wait—you'll find out as we continue to film this exciting episode.

> By the way, are you wondering where Daniel is? Look back at Daniel 2:49 on page 142. WHERE is Daniel?

_____

Daniel is not with Shadrach, Meshach, and Abed-nego in Dura. He is in Babylon at the king's court.

Don't forget to practice your memory verse. This verse shows us just how brave our three teenagers are! Would you have the courage to say this if you knew it would cost you your life? Think about it, and we'll see you back on the set tomorrow.

DAY THREE

SCENE THREE: A RAGING KING

You did a great job helping Mr. Morgan, our sound engineer, yesterday. Today Aunt Sherry needs you to help our cameraman, Mr. Grayson, as he captures the anger and rage of a very proud king. Ask God for His direction, and then zoom in to find out what happens as our three teenagers are brought before the king.

Turn to page 144. Read Daniel 3:14-18 and mark your key words listed on page 56 for these verses on your Observation Worksheets or use your key-word bookmark.

Don't forget to mark your pronouns!

> Daniel 3:14 WHAT does Nebuchadnezzar ask Shadrach, Meshach, and Abed-nego?
>
> "Is it true, that you do not _____ _____ _____
> or _____ the golden _____ that I have
> set up?"

Daniel 3:15 WHAT does King Nebuchnezzar tell Shadrach, Meshach, and Abed-nego will happen to them if they don't worship the image?

_____

Daniel 3:16 HOW do Shadrach, Meshach, and Abed-nego answer the king?

_____

Isn't that awesome? Look at how brave these three guys are! The king could immediately put them to death. But they tell the king they don't need to give him an answer. Their actions have spoken their answer. They did not bow down. They were the only ones left standing when the music played. The king has his answer.

WHY would Shadrach, Meshach, and Abed-nego refuse to bow down to King Nebuchadnezzar's image? Do you know? Let's look up Exodus 20:1-6. God is giving Moses the Ten Commandments.

Exodus 20:3 WHAT is the first commandment?

_____

Exodus 20:4 WHAT did God tell them they were not to make?

_____

Exodus 20:5 WHAT did God tell them they were not to do?

_____

WHY were they not to worship them? WHAT does God tell them about Himself?

"I am a _____ _____."

Shadrach, Meshach, and Abed-nego knew God, they knew

His commandments, and they loved and worshiped the one and only true God!

Turn back to Daniel 3 on page 144.

> Daniel 3:17 WHAT did they tell Nebuchadnezzar about God?
>
> "Our God whom we _____ is _____
> to _____ us."
>
> Daniel 3:18 WHAT else do they tell the king?
>
> "But even if He _____ _____, _____ it
> be _____ to you, O king, that we are _____
> going to _____ your _____ or _____
> the golden _____ that you have set up."

Wow! Just look at Shadrach, Meshach, and Abed-nego's faith and courage. Look at what they say: "Our God is able to deliver us." They know that God has the power to deliver them from the blazing fire, and that He will deliver them out of the king's hand.

But they also say, "Even if He does not…" Why do Shadrach, Meshach, and Abed-nego say this if they know God is able to deliver them? They know that God has the power to deliver, but they also know that God may choose not to. Sometimes God puts us in a fiery furnace to test our faith, to purify us, to make us more like Jesus (James 1:2-4).

God is able to deliver us from hard times, from sickness, and from death, but sometimes God chooses to let us go through these things to fulfill His purpose for our lives and to make us more like Jesus. Have you ever known someone who had cancer but was healed? How about someone else who had cancer and died? Sometimes God delivers us from the fire, sometimes He brings us through the fire, and then sometimes He delivers us into heaven. God is God, and He chooses the outcome.

Shadrach, Meshach, and Abed-nego trust God, even if it means they will go into the blazing fire, even if they die. They choose whom they will worship. They counted the cost of belonging to God. They chose to serve Him no matter the cost.

Look at their words: "Let it be known." They are saying "This is what we believe. These are our convictions. We have made up our minds. We will not change our beliefs. We will not conform. We will not do what everybody else is doing. We will not bend the knee. We will do what God says is right."

When we ask Jesus into our lives to be our Savior, He gets all of us. We totally belong to Him and not to ourselves anymore. We tell God, "You can do with me as You please." There will be kids who will want you to talk like them, listen to the music they listen to, and wear the same kinds of clothes that they wear. They will pressure you to be like them instead of like Jesus.

WHAT will you do? Have you made up your mind? Will you "let it be known"? Or will you bend the knee and be like everyone else? Take some time and think about what you believe, what your standards are. For example, will you listen to music that has bad words? Will you talk like everyone else, even if the words don't please God? Will you dress to be cool and popular, even if the clothing reveals too much or has a bad saying on it?

Write out your standards:

_____

_____

_____

_____

_____

_____

Ask yourself, "Am I willing to live my life to please Jesus, not other people? Even if I am made fun of, called names, left out, or even have to die for what I believe, I will not bend. I will not bow. I will count the cost and follow Jesus." Be like

Shadrach, Meshach, and Abed-nego. Count the cost and decide that your life belongs to Jesus!

Way to go! What an awesome and intense scene. WHAT will happen when we film the next scene in this exciting episode? HOW will King Nebuchadnezzar react to Shadrach, Meshach, and Abed-nego's stand not to serve his gods or worship the golden image? You'll see! Now don't forget to practice your memory verse.

DAY FOUR

SCENE FOUR: A BLAZING FURNACE

"Wow," Max exclaimed as he looked around the set. "What is going on, Aunt Sherry?"

Aunt Sherry smiled as she pointed out the art director and stunt coordinator who were planning the next scene using special effects. "They are getting ready for us to shoot our next scene. It's going to be so cool. You get to watch them use a blue screen to film our characters. When a blue screen is used, only the characters are photographed by the camera. Then later the characters will be inserted into our scene of the fiery furnace using the computer to make it look like they are really there. You won't believe how awesome it is until you see it."

"That sounds amazing," Molly replied.

"Why don't you grab your scripts and finish marking them while we get ready to film?"

"That's a great idea, Aunt Sherry," said Max. "I'll pray, Molly, and then we can get to work."

All right! Now turn to page 145. Yesterday we left Shadrach, Meshach, and Abed-nego as they "let it be known" to

Nebuchadnezzar that they would not bow to, serve, or worship his gods and the image he had set up.

Read Daniel 3:19-26 and mark the key words listed on page 56 in these verses or use your key-word bookmark. Don't forget to mark your pronouns!

Now let's get ready to film this exciting scene. We're ready to roll. Play back music. Stand by... Ask those 5 W's and an H and direct King Nebuchadnezzar.

Daniel 3:19 HOW does Nebuchadnezzar react to Shadrach, Meshach, and Abed-nego's answer?

He was filled with _____ .

WHAT are his lines?

He gave orders to _____

_____ .

Wow! Look at how angry the king is. He wants the furnace heated seven times more than it was usually heated.

Daniel 3:20 WHAT were his commands?

_____

_____

Daniel 3:21-22 WHAT happened to the men who carried up Shadrach, Meshach, and Abed-nego and threw them in?

_____

_____

_____

_____

Draw a picture in the box below to show this amazing scene.

Daniel 3:23 WHAT do we see about Shadrach, Meshach, and Abed-nego as they are thrown into the fire?

_____

Daniel 3:24-25 WHAT does Nebuchadnezzar see?

HOW many were thrown in?

_____

HOW many were in the furnace?

_____

HOW does Nebuchadnezzar describe this fourth one?

_____

WHO was the fourth? Do you have any idea?

_____

Do you know who this fourth one is that Nebuchadnezzar says looks like "a son of the gods"? Most Bible scholars think that this is Jesus before He left heaven and came to earth as a baby in the New Testament. Sometimes in the Old Testament before Jesus was born, He would make appearances on Earth.

Draw a picture of Daniel 3:24-25 in the box to show what this exciting scene will look like on film.

Daniel 3:26 WHAT does Nebuchadnezzar say to Shadrach, Meshach, and Abed-nego?

_____

Are you *amazed* that Jesus was with our three awesome teen-agers in the midst of the fire? Remember, when we invite Jesus into our lives, Jesus comes to live in us (John 14:23). Jesus will be with us no matter what we go through.

What will Shadrach, Meshach, and Abed-nego look like when they come out of the furnace, since we saw the valiant warriors who threw them in burned up? Will there be any marks or burns on them? Will they smell like smoke? We'll find out.

SCENE FIVE: SERVANTS OF GOD MOST HIGH

WHAT an awesome scene! We can't wait to see this episode once Miss Lenyer, our digital artist, has added in all those cool special effects. Today we need to film our final scene in this episode. Pray and then pull out your scripts.

Turn to page 146. Read Daniel 3:27-30 and mark the key words listed on page 56 in these verses or use your key-word bookmark.

Don't forget to mark your pronouns! And mark anything that tells you WHERE by double-underlining the <u><u>WHERE</u></u> in green.

Now help Mr. Jackson with the makeup to show what our three teenagers look like as they come out of the fire. Ask those 5 W's and an H.

> Daniel 3:27 WHAT did the king's high officials see about Shadrach, Meshach, and Abed-nego?
>
> _____
>
> _____

Isn't that cool? Here they are in the middle of the fire, and there is no effect of the fire on them: no burns, no singed hair, no smell of the fire. God is so *awesome!*

> Daniel 3:28 HOW does Nebuchadnezzar react? WHAT does he say?
>
> "_____ be the _____ of _____,
> _____, and _____."

> WHOM did Nebuchadnezzar say God sent to deliver His servants?
>
> _____

Daniel 3:28 WHY were they delivered?

_____

WHAT did Shadrach, Meshach, and Abed-nego do?

They y __ __ __ __ __ up their _____ so
as not to _____ or _____ any _____
except their own _____.

Look at our brave teenagers' witness to a proud king! They are willing to go against the king, to give up their lives in order to not worship anyone but the one true God! Incredible!

Daniel 3:29 WHAT is Nebuchadnezzar's decree?

_____

WHAT will happen if they speak anything offensive against God?

_____

WHAT does Nebuchadnezzar say about God?

_____

Wow! Nebuchadnezzar recognizes there is no other god like God!

Daniel 3:30 WHAT happened to Shadrach, Meshach, and Abed-nego?

_____

Look at how God honored their faith. When you go through the fire and God purifies you to be more like Jesus, then He can use you in ways you never dreamed possible. On the lines below, write a prayer to God and ask Him to work in your life so He can use you:

_____

_____

_____

Cut and print! That was good! Way to go! We can't wait to see this exciting episode. You have done an awesome job this week! Don't forget to say your memory verse to a grown-up. Ask that person what he or she is willing to "let it be known" about him or her. See you back on the set next week.

4

A VISION OF A STRONG TREE

DANiEL 4

Wow! Were you shocked last week when you saw King Nebuchadnezzar create a golden image and decide that everyone must worship it or die? Three brave young men let it be known they would not bend their knees so they ended up in a fiery furnace and were delivered by God. WHAT a suspenseful episode! WHAT will happen next? Grab those scripts and let's find out.

DAY ONE

SCENE ONE: NEBUCHADNEZZAR'S PALACE

"Wow, Aunt Sherry, those special effects are so cool!" Molly exclaimed as she, Max, and Aunt Sherry finished watching the completed episode on the fiery furnace.

"It sure was!" Max joined in. "I can't get over how incredible those scenes are of the men being incinerated into ashes as they throw Shadrach, Meshach, and Abed-nego into the fiery furnace."

"It's pretty amazing what you can do with special effects,"

Aunt Sherry replied. "Are you ready to head back to the set and mark those scripts?"

"We sure are," Max replied. "Let's go, Molly."

Now that we are back on the set, don't forget to pray. Then turn to page 146. Read Daniel 4:1-9 and mark the key words listed below on your Observation Worksheets. Add any new key words to your key-word bookmark.

Key-Word List for Daniel 4

God (Most High, King of heaven) (draw a purple triangle and color it yellow)

Daniel (Belteshazzar) (color it blue)

dream (vision) (draw a blue cloud around it)

Nebuchadnezzar (color it orange)

kingdom (draw a purple crown and color it blue)

sin (iniquities) (color it brown)

Don't forget to mark your pronouns! And mark anything that tells WHEN by drawing a green clock 🕐 or green circle like this: ◯ .

All right! Now that our scripts are marked, let's find out what is happening in chapter 4. Ask those 5 W's and an H.

Daniel 4:1-4 WHO is writing this chapter? WHO is speaking?

_____

_____

_____

Daniel 4:2 WHAT is King Nebuchadnezzar doing?

_____

Are you surprised to see King Nebuchadnezzar declaring these things about God? Make a list in the box below to show what you learned about God in verses 2-3.

What I Learned About God

Daniel 4:4 WHERE is Nebuchadnezzar?

_____

Daniel 4:5 WHAT does Nebuchadnezzar see?

_____

HOW does Nebuchadnezzar react to this vision?

_____

Daniel 4:6 WHOM does Nebuchadnezzar bring into his presence?

_____

WHY does he send for them?

_____

_____

Daniel 4:7 Can they tell Nebuchadnezzar what the dream means?

_____

Daniel 4:8 WHOM does Nebuchadnezzar send for next?

_____

Daniel 4:9 WHAT does Nebuchadnezzar say about Daniel?

"O Belteshazzar, _____ of the _____...
a _____ of the _____ _____ is in you
and no _____ baffles you."

Isn't it fantastic the way Nebuchadnezzar sees that Daniel has a different spirit in him? Will Daniel (Belteshazzar) be able to tell the king his dream? We'll find out as we finish this scene tomorrow. But before we leave the set, we need to discover our new memory verse.

Look at the three rolls of film on the next page. One of these three rolls gives you the correct words for your memory verse this week. To find the correct roll of film, look through Daniel 4 on pages 146-151 and at the book on page 77.

Find which roll of film's words fit the blanks on the script. Then circle that roll of film and fill in the blanks with the correct words to complete your verse. Don't forget to write down the reference. Practice this verse three times today!

Way to go! You did it!

Now, I Nebuchadnezzar, _____,

_____, and _____ the _____

of _____, for all His _____ are

_____ and His _____ _____,

and He is _____ to _____ those

who _____ in _____ .

Daniel 4: _____

SCENE TWO: NEBUCHADNEZZAR'S DREAM

"Hey, guys, are you ready to find out what Nebuchadnezzar dreams that has him so fearful?" Aunt Sherry asked Max and Molly as they headed onto the set.

"We can't wait!" Molly replied. "It must be some dream to alarm this arrogant king."

"Wait until we film it. It is going to look so cool with Miss Lenyer's special effects. But first I want to give you and Max a chance to create a set of storyboards."

"What are storyboards?" Max asked.

"Storyboards are sketches of the main scenes in our television show. I want you and Molly to create storyboards for our next scene."

"That sounds like fun," Max replied. "Let's go."

Now that we're back on the set, don't forget to pray. Then turn to page 147. Read Daniel 4:10-17 and mark your key words listed on page 74 in these verses or use your key-word bookmark.

Don't forget to mark your pronouns! And mark anything that tells WHEN by drawing a green clock 🕐 or green circle like this: ◯.

Daniel 4:10 WHAT was Nebuchadnezzar's vision?

_____

Daniel 4:11 WHAT do we see about this tree?

_____

Daniel 4:12 WHAT do we see about the tree's foliage?

_____

_____

WHAT does the tree provide for the beasts, birds, and living creatures?

_____

Now create your first storyboard by sketching the scene in Daniel 4:10-12 in the box below.

Daniel 4:13 WHAT does Nebuchadnezzar see descend from heaven?

_____

Daniel 4:14 WHAT does this angelic watcher shout out?

"_____ _____ the tree and _____ _____ its _____, _____ off its _____ and _____ its _____; let the _____ flee from under it and the _____ from its _____."

Draw this storyboard for Daniel 4:13-14 in the box below.

Daniel 4:15 WHAT else did the angelic watcher shout out?

"Leave the _____ with its _____ in the ground, but with a _____ of _____ and _____ around it... and let him be drenched with the _____ of _____, and let him _____ with the _____ in the _____ of the _____."

Daniel 4:16 "Let his _____ be _____ from that of a _____ and let a _____ _____ be given to him, and let _____ _____ of time pass over him."

Create your next storyboard by sketching Daniel 4:15-16 in the box on the next page.

```



```

Outstanding artwork! Now look at Daniel 4:17.

WHY does Nebuchadnezzar receive this dream? WHAT are the living to know?

"That the _____ _____ is _____ over the realm of _____, and _____ it on whom He _____ and sets over it the _____ of _____."

WHAT does it mean that God is God Most High? The Hebrew name for God Most High is *El Elyon* (pronounced *el el-YON*). This is the name of God that shows us that God is the Possessor of heaven and earth. God is sovereign. *Sovereign* means that God is the Ruler over *everything!* There is absolutely nothing that God doesn't have control over! Amazing!

Are you curious about King Nebuchadnezzar's unusual dream? WHAT could this tree and it being chopped down mean?

Don't forget to practice your memory verse. See you on the set tomorrow!

DAY THREE

SCENE THREE: DANIEL INTERPRETS THE DREAM

It's great to have you back! Miss Anna, the production manager, needs your help to make sure everyone is where they're supposed to be. Why don't you get on the walkie-talkie and make sure King Nebuchadnezzar and Daniel are ready for our next scene?

Don't forget to pray. Then turn to page 149. Read Daniel 4:18-27 and mark the key words listed on page 74 in these verses or use your key-word bookmark.

Don't forget to mark your pronouns! And mark anything that tells WHEN by drawing a green clock 🕐 or green circle like this: ○.

Great work! Quiet on the set! Camera One, pick up on Daniel. Come in tight. We need a close-up as he responds to the king's dream.

Daniel 4:19 HOW did Daniel react to the king's dream?

He was _____; his thoughts _____ him.

Daniel 4:20-22 WHOM does the tree represent in the dream?

_____

Daniel 4:22 WHAT does Daniel say this tree shows us about the king?

Bring on Neb

"You have become _____ and grown _____,
and your _____ has become great and reached
to the sky and your _____ to the end of the
_____."

Daniel 4:23-25 WHAT is going to happen to Nebuchadnezzar? WHAT is the decree of the Most High to
the king?

"That you be _____ away from _____
and your _____ place be with the _____
of the field, and you be given _____ to _____
like cattle and be drenched with the _____ of
_____; and _____ _____ of time will
pass over you."

Daniel 4:25 Until WHEN? WHAT is King Nebuchad-nezzar to recognize?

"That the _____ _____ is _____
over the realm of _____ and _____
it on whomever He _____."

Daniel 4:26 WHY is the stump with the roots of the tree left?

To show Nebuchadnezzar that his _____ will
be assured to him after he recognizes that it is _____
_____ that _____.

Daniel 4:27 WHAT is Daniel's advice to Nebuchadnezzar?

"Break away now from your _____ by
doing _____. Show _____ to the _____."

Does this sound like good news or bad news for King
Nebuchadnezzar?   ___ Good   ___ Bad

Wow! Can you believe this dream? God starts off showing Nebuchadnezzar how awesome his kingdom is. The tree is strong and fruitful. Then God shows him that he will be driven from mankind until he recognizes that there is a Most High, the Ruler of mankind, who bestows power on whomever He wishes.

Daniel gives the king great advice: "Break away from your sins and do righteousness." God is giving the king a chance to change his ways and his heart and to recognize that God is the Giver of his kingdom. All that he has is from the Most High. There is a Ruler over all, and it's not King Nebuchadnezzar. It's El Elyon—God Most High!

Cut and print! Now use all the words from each of the blanks on pages 82-84 and circle them in the word search on the next page. If a word is used more than once, you only need to circle it one time.

N	D	K	S	H	R	M	A	J	E	S	T	Y	N
E	E	U	D	Q	U	O	P	D	S	M	R	E	S
V	M	B	X	W	L	S	P	O	E	I	V	N	S
I	R	D	U	P	E	T	A	M	H	E	I	V	E
R	A	N	V	C	S	L	L	I	S	S	Z	A	N
D	L	I	K	W	H	Q	L	N	I	S	T	H	S
Y	A	K	P	E	O	A	E	I	W	P	M	I	U
K	I	N	G	D	O	M	D	O	N	T	E	G	O
B	E	A	S	T	S	M	T	N	H	G	R	H	E
R	P	M	G	R	A	S	S	E	E	E	C	D	T
S	D	O	I	R	E	P	X	I	A	Z	Y	R	H
H	V	C	R	B	O	N	C	T	V	R	Z	A	G
A	R	T	A	O	V	R	U	L	E	R	T	A	I
E	Q	E	R	I	S	T	R	O	N	G	J	H	R

Way to go! We are so proud of you! Will Nebuchadnezzar change? Will he break away from his sins? You'll find out. Don't forget to practice your memory verse.

DAY FOUR

SCENE FOUR: BABYLON THE GREAT

You did a wonderful job helping Miss Anna out yesterday. Today we have a very cool assignment for you. You get to help Mr. Jackson, the makeup artist, get Nebuchadnezzar transformed for a very unbelievable scene. But before you head to the makeup room, turn to page 150.

Read Daniel 4:28-33 and mark the key words listed on page 74 in these verses or use your key-word bookmark.

Don't forget to mark your pronouns! And mark anything that tells you WHERE by double-underlining the <u>WHERE</u> in green. Mark anything that tells you WHEN by drawing a green clock or green circle like this: ◯.

Now that your scripts are marked, ask the 5 W's and an H. After that you can show WHAT happens to King Nebuchadnezzar by drawing the storyboards for these two scenes.

> Daniel 4:29-30 WHAT was King Nebuchadnezzar saying as he walked around the roof of his palace?
>
> "Is this not _____ the great, which I myself have _____ as a royal _____ by the might of my _____ and for the _____ of my _____?"

Take a look at Miss Anna's production notes in the box to see why King Nebuchadnezzar was so proud of his city and palace.

PRODUCTION MANAGER'S NOTES

Babylon the Great

Did you know that Babylon covered 20 square miles? It had two gigantic walls to protect it. The inner wall was so wide that two chariots could fit side by side. Babylon could be entered through eight different gates. The most famous gate was the northern Ishtar Gate, which was decorated with dragons and bulls in enameled bricks. And the road to this gate had high walls that were decorated with lions. Inside this gate was the main palace that Nebuchadnezzar built.

The city of Babylon was famous for its hanging gardens that

Nebuchadnezzar built for one of his queens who was home-sick for her country. These hanging gardens are one of the seven wonders of the world. Nebuchadnezzar was the greatest king of the neo-Babylonian period and the last great ruler of Babylon.*

WHOM is Nebuchadnezzar praising for all he has? Circle one:

        a. God   b. Himself

Daniel 4:31 WHAT does the voice from heaven say?

"_____ has been _____ from you."

Draw this fantastic scene from Daniel 4:28-32 in the box below.

* Holman Bible Publishers, *Holman Illustrated Bible Dictionary* (Nashville: Holman Bible Publishers, 2003), pp. 158-59.

Daniel 4:33 WHAT happened? Did Nebuchadnezzar's dream come true? Was he driven from mankind? Did he lose his reason and his kingdom for seven periods of time?

_____

_____

Draw this very unusual and amazing scene of Daniel 4:33 in the box below.

Wow! Can you believe it? God gave Nebuchadnezzar 12 months from the time Daniel interpreted his dream to turn from his sins. What a patient God! But WHAT does Nebuchadnezzar do? Instead of recognizing WHO God is, he shows his pride in all his accomplishments, his kingdom, and his power.

Nebuchadnezzar had built an awesome kingdom of beautiful hanging gardens, gigantic walls decorated with lions, and gates decorated with dragons and bulls. Twelve months later we see Nebuchadnezzar walking around on the roof of the palace and bragging about what an awesome palace and kingdom he has built.

But God showed him WHO the King really is. Immediately Nebuchadnezzar was driven from mankind, eating grass like the cattle. WHAT will happen next? Will King Nebuchadnezzar be driven from mankind for the rest of his life, eating grass like the cattle, having hair like eagles' feathers, and sporting nails like birds' claws? You'll find out. Don't forget to practice your memory verse!

SCENE FIVE: A HUMBLED KING

"Thanks, Aunt Sherry, for letting us help Mr. Jackson transform King Nebuchadnezzar into a beast with hair like eagles' feathers and nails like birds' claws," Molly said as Aunt Sherry walked up.

Max joined in. "That was the coolest. It is so amazing how makeup can transform a man into a beast. We are having a great time."

"Well, I'm proud of you for all your hard work marking scripts, running lines, and especially for studying God's Word. Are you ready to find out what happens to King Nebuchadnezzar?"

"We sure are!" Max and Molly laughed as they spoke at the same time.

"Great! I'll pray and then we'll pull out our scripts."

Turn to page 151. Read Daniel 4:34-37 and mark your key words listed on page 74 in these verses or use your key-word bookmark.

Don't forget to mark your pronouns! And mark anything that tells you WHEN by drawing a green clock or green circle like this: ⭕ .

> Daniel 4:34 WHEN did Nebuchadnezzar have his reason return to him?
>
> _____
>
> _____
>
> Daniel 4:36 WHAT did God restore to Nebuchadnezzar?
>
> _____
>
> _____
>
> Daniel 4:37 WHY did God cause Nebuchadnezzar to lose his reason and his kingdom? WHAT is God able to do?
>
> _____
>
> Draw this scene from Daniel 4:34-37 in the box below.

Make a list of the things you learned about God in Daniel 4:32-37.

What I Learned About God

WHAT an *awesome* God! Look at verse 35 and see all that God is over. He is over the host of heaven and all the inhabitants of the earth. Draw a picture in the box below to show everything that God is over.

Amazing! God is over *everything!* Nebuchadnezzar was driven from mankind for seven periods of time until he raised his eyes to heaven to recognize, bless, and praise God Most High!

Nebuchadnezzar was humbled. He finally got it. Nebuchadnezzar finally saw who God is: not just another god, not just Daniel's God, but El Elyon, God Most High and Ruler over everything. And God restored to him the glory of his kingdom.

God is the only One to be worshiped and praised. In Isaiah 42:8, God says He will not give His glory to another. God created us. He gives us our gifts and abilities. We are not to brag about the things we do. We are to give God the honor and glory.

HOW about you? Do you honor and praise God—or yourself? Do you brag about your sports ability, about how smart and talented you are, or about your looks? Write out the gifts that God has given you and tell how you handle those gifts. Also tell if there is anything you need to change.

_____

_____

_____

_____

Remember: God humbles those who walk in pride. Don't be like Nebuchadnezzar. Praise God for all that He has given you! Every good and perfect gift comes from God (James 1:17).

Awesome work! Don't forget to say your memory verse out loud to a grown-up, and ask that person if he or she sees any pride in you. If the grown-up says yes, go to God and ask Him to help you be humble like Daniel.

5

HaNDWRiTiNG ON THE WaLL

DANiEL 5

What an amazing week as we filmed a very arrogant and proud king driven from mankind, eating grass like the cattle, with hair like eagles' feathers and nails like birds' claws. Mr. Jackson did an awesome job as he made up King Nebuchadnezzar. Were you surprised to see this mighty king finally humble himself before God Most High? Have you humbled yourself and thanked God for all the gifts He has given you? Way to go! We are so proud of you! What will happen in our new episode this week? Let's head back to the set to find out.

DaY ONE

A CHANGE OF KiNG

"Come on in," Miss Lenyer called out to Max and Molly. "Did Sherry tell you about the awesome scene we will be filming today?"

"No," replied Max. "We have to mark our scripts to find out."

Miss Lenyer laughed at Max's answer. "All right, you and

Molly better get started. You don't want to miss this incredible scene."

Let's ask God for His help. Then we need to turn to page 152. Read Daniel 5:1-6 and mark the key words listed below on your Observation Worksheets. Add any new key words to your key-word bookmark.

Key Words for Daniel 5

God (Most High God, Lord) (draw a purple triangle and color it yellow)

Belshazzar (color it pink)

vessels (color it yellow)

Daniel (color it blue)

kingdom (draw a purple crown and color it blue)

Don't forget to mark your pronouns! And mark anything that tells you WHERE by double-underlining the WHERE in green. Mark anything that tells you WHEN by drawing a green clock or green circle like this:◯.

Now that your scripts are marked, let's film our next scene.

Daniel 5:1 WHO is the king? WHAT's the king's name?

_____

We have a new king of Babylon. King Nebuchadnezzar died in 562 BC. It is now 539 BC, and Daniel is around 80 years old. Take a look at Miss Anna's background information on this new king, Belshazzar.

PRODUCTION MANAGER'S NOTES

BELSHAZZAR

Did you know that the mention of this king, Belshazzar, used to make some people think that the Bible was not true because they could not find a king of Babylon listed in history named Belshazzar?

Historical accounts listed Nabondius as the last king of Babylon, but the Bible listed a king named Belshazzar. Guess what happened? In the nineteenth century there was an archaeological dig that proved that God's Word was right. There were inscriptions that showed there was a king of Babylon named Belshazzar.

So WHO is Belshazzar? Belshazzar was the son of Nabondius, who became king of Babylon in 556 BC. Because Nabondius was more interested in historical research than in ruling Babylon, he appointed his son Belshazzar as his co-regent. That means they shared being king of Babylon.

In Daniel 5 you will see Nebuchadnezzar referred to as Belshazzar's father. Most scholars believe this is because it was proper (court etiquette) to call Belshazzar the son of King Nebuchadnezzar, even though he was not Belshazzar's father. Belshazzar was a legal heir of King Nebuchadnezzar and is regarded as "the son." Also, in ancient Oriental languages the word FATHER was used to refer to any male ancestor. Remember, Belshazzar's father is Nabondius, his co-regent.*

---

* John Phillips and Jerry Vines, *Exploring the Book of Daniel* (Neptune, NJ: Loizeaux Brothers, 1990), pp. 79, app. 16.

Now that we know something about our new king, help Mr. Andy get the props in place so we can start filming our new episode.

Daniel 5:1 WHAT is happening? WHAT is King Belshazzar holding?

A g _ _ _ _   f_ _ _ _

Daniel 5:2-3 WHAT does Belshazzar order to be brought to the feast for the king, his nobles, his wives, and his concubines to drink from?

_____

WHERE were these vessels from?

_____

Daniel 5:4 WHAT did they do as they drank from these holy vessels of God?

_____

_____

Now think about this for a minute. These vessels are the ones that King Nebuchadnezzar brought out of God's temple when he captured Jerusalem. These vessels belonged to the Most High God and were used for temple worship, and here these people are partying, praising the false gods of gold, silver, bronze, iron, wood, and stone.

HOW do you think God feels about His vessels being used to praise another god?

_____

_____

Daniel 5:5 WHAT happened?

_____

_____

_____

Draw a picture of this shocking event in the box below.

Daniel 5:6 HOW did the king react?

_____

Wow! Does this scene give you a clue to how God felt about the king using His holy vessels to praise false gods? Tomorrow we will find out how treating God's vessels as holy applies to you.

Now discover your memory verse for this week by looking at the handwriting on the wall that Miss Lenyer helped Max and Molly create using the inverse alphabet code on the next page.

To decode this message, find the letter of the alphabet that represents the letter written in the message. The first letter in our message on the wall is the letter *Y*. Look at the inverse alphabet code under the letter *Y* and write the letter that *Y* is representing, which is the letter *B*, on the line under the message on the wall. Do the same thing for each letter until you have uncovered God's message, your memory verse for this week. Then find the reference by reading Daniel 5.

Inverse Alphabet Code

A B C D E F G H I J K L M N O P Q R S T U V W X Y Z
| | | | | | | | | | | | | | | | | | | | | | | | | |
Z Y X W V U T S R Q P O N M L K J I H G F E D C B A

_____ ___ ___ __ _____
YFG   GSV   TLW   RM   DSLHV

_____ ___ ____ _____
SZMW   ZIV   BLFI   ORUV-YIVZGS

_____ ____ _____, ____
ZMW   BLFI   DZBH,   BLF

_____ ____ _____.
SZEV   MLG   TOLIRURVW.

Daniel 5: ____ b

Way to go! Now practice this verse three times today!

GOD'S HOLY VESSELS

Yesterday was a little scary as we watched King Belshazzar throw a huge party and use God's holy vessels to praise false gods of gold, silver, bronze, iron, wood, and stone.

HOW did God react? A hand appeared and began writing on the wall of the king's palace. Look at King Belshazzar's reaction: His face grew pale, his thoughts alarmed him, his hip joints went slack, and his knees began knocking together. Do you think that drinking and praising other gods using God's holy vessels is treating God as holy, as God Most High, the Ruler over everything?

So HOW does this apply to you? HOW can you treat God and His vessels as holy? Let's find out. Talk to God, and then pull out your script, your Bible. Today we are going to find out how you can honor God and His holy vessels.

Look up and read 1 Corinthians 6:19-20.

1 Corinthians 6:19 WHAT is our body if we are believers in Jesus Christ?

_____

WHO is in us? _____

Do we belong to ourselves? _____

1 Corinthians 6:20 WHY don't we belong to ourselves?

We have been _____ with a _____.

Do you know what that price is? It's Jesus' death on a cross to save us from our sins. Once we accept Jesus Christ as our

Savior, we no longer belong to ourselves. Our bodies are a temple of God, a holy vessel for Him to use.

Have you accepted Jesus Christ as your Savior? If you haven't invited Jesus into your life and you want to, the first thing you need to do is believe that Jesus is our Savior, that He is God's Son. He is God, and He lived a perfect life without sin and died on a cross to pay for our sins. Then He was buried, and God raised Him from the dead.

You also have to know that you are a sinner and be willing to confess those sins to God and turn away from them. You have to be willing to turn your entire life over to God and to follow Jesus.

You can pray a prayer like this:

Thank You, God, for loving me and sending Your Son, Jesus Christ, to die for my sins. I am sorry for the things I have done wrong. I am repenting, changing my mind about my sins. Sin is wrong. I don't want to do things my way anymore. I want to receive Jesus Christ as my Savior, and now I turn my entire life over to You. Amen.

If you prayed this prayer, you are a part of God's family! You are God's child, and Jesus and the Holy Spirit will come to live in you (John 14:23). You are a temple of the Holy Spirit. You belong to God!

Now look back at 1 Corinthians 6:20. WHAT are we to do?

_____ God in

your _____.

To glorify God is to honor and praise Him. Think about it. You are a holy vessel of God. HOW do you live? Do you praise God with your life, or does your life show that you are praising the things that are in this world?

Ask yourself: "Am I careful with my eyes? WHAT kinds of movies do I watch, and WHAT kind of books and magazines do I read?"

"HOW do I use my mouth? Do I tell bad jokes? Do I make fun of other people? Do I use bad words or slang that don't show I belong to God? Do I encourage other people with my words? Do I smoke or drink? Do I eat healthy foods?"

> Write out how you use your mouth and what you need to change:

"HOW do I use my ears? Do I listen to music with bad lyrics? Do I listen when kids make fun of or talk about other kids, or do I tell them to stop and then walk away?"

> Write out how you use your ears and if you need to change what you listen to:

"HOW do I use my hands? Do I help other people? Do I help someone at school with homework? Do I help Mom around the house? Do I ever hit my brother or sister? Do I help any older people by raking their yards? Do I take food to the needy?"

> Write out one way you can use your hands to honor God by loving other people:

"HOW do I use my feet? Do I go places that Mom and Dad wouldn't want me to go? Do I make friends with a kid who is lonely? Which parties and friends' houses do I go to? Do I visit older people who are lonely? Do I go to church activities?"

Tell how you use your feet:

_____

"HOW do I dress my body?" If you are a girl, do you dress in short skirts and shirts that show too much? If you are a guy, do you wear shirts that say inappropriate things and jeans that barely stay on?

Does how you dress show other people that you belong to Jesus?

_____

Name one way you can keep God's temple (your body) holy:

_____

Way to go! We are so proud of you.

WHAT will happen when we head back to the set tomorrow? Will there be anyone who can tell King Belshazzar what this hand has written on the wall? We'll find out. Don't forget to practice your memory verse!

DAY THREE

CALL IN THE WISE MEN

Hey, it's great to have you back on the set! You did a fantastic job yesterday as you learned how to keep God's holy vessel, your body, holy. Today you need to help Mr. Jackson get Belshazzar ready as we film his next scene. Remember what he looked like as we left him in Daniel 5:6? Apply Belshazzar's makeup.

Then turn to page 152. Read Daniel 5:7-12 and mark the key words on page 94 listed in these verses or use your key-word bookmark. Don't forget to mark your pronouns!

Ready on the set! Let's film our next scene.

Daniel 5:7 WHOM did the king call for?

_____

WHAT did the king offer the one who could interpret this inscription?

"He shall be clothed with _____ and have a _____ of _____… and have authority as _____ _____."

Why third ruler? Remember, there are already two rulers: King Belshazzar and his father, King Nabondius.

Daniel 5:8 Could the king's wise men interpret the inscription?

_____

Daniel 5:9 HOW did this affect King Belshazzar?

_____

_____

(We need more makeup, Mr. Jackson!)

HOW did his nobles react?

_____

Daniel 5:10 WHO enters the banquet hall?

_____

Daniel 5:10-12 WHOM did the queen tell Belshazzar to summon?

_____

WHAT do we learn about Daniel in verses 11-12? Make a list in the box on the next page.

What I Learned About Daniel

Amazing! Will Daniel interpret the handwriting on the wall? Hang in there! You'll find out. Don't forget to practice your memory verse.

DAY FOUR

SEND FOR DANIEL

"That was so cool watching the scene where Miss Lenyer made the hand write on the wall," Molly told Max as they headed to the makeup room to tell Mr. Jackson that Aunt Sherry was ready for Daniel.

"It sure was. Hey, Mr. Jackson," Max called out, "Aunt Sherry is ready for Daniel on the set."

"He's ready to go. How does he look?"

"Wow!" Molly exclaimed. "I can't believe it. He really looks 80 years old."

Mr. Jackson smiled. "It's the magic of Hollywood. We can make you look beautiful, old, or transform you into a monster."

Max and Molly laughed at Mr. Jackson's theatrics. "We'll go tell Aunt Sherry that Daniel is on his way."

All right! Quiet on the set everyone. Let's pray so we can

find out what happens when Daniel comes in to see King Belshazzar. WHAT will Daniel say to this king?

Turn to page 153. Read Daniel 5:13-23 and mark the key words listed on page 94 in these verses or use your key-word bookmark.

Don't forget to mark your pronouns! And mark anything that tells you WHERE by double-underlining the <u>WHERE</u> in green. Mark anything that tells you WHEN by drawing a green clock 🕐 or green circle like this: ○ .

Daniel 5:13 WHAT does Belshazzar ask Daniel?

_____

Daniel 5:14-16 List some of the things Belshazzar says about Daniel.

_____

_____

Daniel 5:16 WHAT will the king give Daniel if he interprets the message?

_____

_____

Daniel 5:17 HOW does Daniel respond to the king's offer?

_____

_____

Isn't that awesome? Daniel will tell him the truth, but not for his own personal benefit, not to increase his wealth or to advance himself. Daniel is still a man of faith, wisdom, and integrity.

Daniel 5:18-21 WHAT does Daniel remind Belshazzar about?

_____

_____

Daniel 5:22 WHAT does Daniel tell Belshazzar?

_____

Daniel 5:23 WHAT did Belshazzar do wrong?

_____

_____

In WHOSE hand is Belshazzar's life-breath? _____

WHOM did he not glorify with his ways? _____

Wow! Just look at what Daniel says to King Belshazzar. Daniel reminds Belshazzar about what happened when King Nebuchadnezzar became proud. He tells him, "You knew all this, and you still did not humble your heart. You didn't learn from King Nebuchadnezzar's mistakes. You put yourself above God. You drank out of God's vessels and praised other gods. You did not glorify God, even though He holds your breath, your very life in His hands."

Now ask yourself, "Do I honor God with the way I live? Do I realize that every breath I take is in His hands, that my life is a gift from God?"

Name one way you can honor and bless God:

_____

How would you like to be given this message? It doesn't sound like the message from the handwriting on the wall is going to be good news, does it? WHAT will God reveal to this king? We'll find out tomorrow.

MENE, MENE, TEKEL, UPHARSIN

Are you ready to film our last scene this week? WHAT will the handwriting on the wall reveal to this arrogant king? Let's find out. Don't forget to talk to God.

Turn to page 155. Read Daniel 5:24-31 and mark the key words listed on page 94 in these verses or use your key-word bookmark.

Don't forget to mark your pronouns! And mark anything that tells you WHEN by drawing a green clock ⏰ or green circle like this: ◯ .

Daniel 5:24 WHO sent the hand that wrote the inscription?

_____

Daniel 5:25-28 WHAT three things did the inscription tell Belshazzar?

1) "_____ has _____ your _____ and put an _____ to it."

2) "You have been _____ on the _____ and
   found _____."

3) "Your _____ has been _____ and
   given over to the _____ and _____."

Whoa! How would you like to get a message like this? God is very, very upset with King Belshazzar. God tells Belshazzar his kingdom is over. He has been found deficient. Belshazzar's kingdom will be divided and given to the Medes and the Persians. Remember Nebuchadnezzar's dream about the statue? Do you remember how God told him he was the head of gold but another kingdom, an inferior kingdom, would take over? Does it sound like that is about to happen?

Daniel 5:29 WHAT happened to Daniel?

_____

_____

Daniel 5:30 WHAT happened to Belshazzar? WHEN did it happen?

_____

Daniel 5:31 WHO receives the kingdom?

_____

Is Nebuchadnezzar's dream about the statue coming true?

_____

Look at Daniel 5:28. WHOM does it say Belshazzar's kingdom is given over to?

_____

God has just shown you the next kingdom on the statue! Why don't you turn back to your picture of the statue on page 49 and in the space next to the silver breast and arms write the name of the next kingdom: Kingdom of Medes and Persians. Isn't that exciting!

Now WHAT does chapter 5 show us about King Belshazzar? Circle all of the descriptions below that you think apply to him.

    a. He was humble.   b. He was a great king.

    c. He was arrogant.   d. He didn't know or honor God.

    e. He mocked God.   f. He was proud.

    g. He placed himself above God by praising other gods with God's holy vessels.

Belshazzar did not learn from King Nebuchadnezzar's mistakes. He thought he was invincible, that nothing could touch him because he was ruling such an awesome kingdom. But Belshazzar found out there is a God who holds man's breath in His hand, and He alone is to be praised.

Ask yourself, "Am I more like Belshazzar or Daniel?"

_____

"Do I think I can do whatever I want to? Or do I live to please God?" Write out what you do, and give an

example of how you are living to have your way or
how you're living to please God:

_____

_____

_____

_____

_____

_____

All right! As you leave the set this week, don't forget to say
your memory verse to a grown-up. Ask God to show you when
you are walking in pride, and to help you glorify Him in all
your ways!

6

CAST INTO THE LIONS' DEN

DANiEL 6

Wow! What did you think about King Belshazzar and that scary handwriting on the wall with its message of doom for this king? Would you ever dishonor God the way he did? Remember, we are God's holy vessels. Our lives are to praise Him!

Are you ready to find out what happens to Daniel next? Let's head back to the set and find out what happens with the new king.

DAY ONE

CAST CHANGE

"Okay! Places, everybody. Is Darius ready for our next scene?" Aunt Sherry called out. "Good. Bring him out. Okay, Mr. Grayson, we'll start with Camera Two. We're ready to roll. Quiet on the set! Let's pray. Stand by...action!"

Turn to page 156, to our opening scene. Read Daniel 6:1-5 and mark the key words listed on the next page in your Observation Worksheets. Add any new key words to your key-word bookmark.

Key-Word List for Daniel 6

God (draw a purple triangle and color it yellow)

Daniel (color it blue)

kingdom (draw a purple crown and color it blue)

praying (petition) (draw a purple ⌣ and color it pink)

deliver (draw a blue ⌣ and color it red)

Don't forget to mark your pronouns!

Now WHO is in our opening scene?

Daniel 6:1-2 WHO is the king?

_____

Remember, we saw Darius take over the kingdom of Babylon in Daniel 5:30-31. The head of gold has fallen, and now the Medes and Persians (the breast and arms of silver) are in control of Babylon.

Daniel 6:2 HOW does Darius set up the kingdom?

He appoints _____ _____ over the kingdom and he puts t__ __ __ e c__ __ __ __ __ __ __ __ __ __ __ s over these satraps.

King Darius' kingdom was so large that he needed help to watch over his people and wealth. So he appointed satraps. Satraps were like governors. They were in charge of areas called provinces. The satraps reported to commissioners. Commissioners were like vice presidents. They made sure the satraps did their jobs, and they managed large areas, probably made up of many provinces. The king would be like a president…except he wasn't elected! He was sovereign and could do anything he wanted to.

WHO is one of the three commissioners?

_____

Remember, Daniel is over 80 years old.

Daniel 6:3 HOW well did Daniel do his job?

_____

WHAT did the king plan to appoint Daniel over?

_____

Amazing! Daniel does such an awesome job that the king is going to set him over the entire kingdom. Let's find out how the other commissioners and satraps feel about that.

Daniel 6:4 WHAT did these other commissioners and satraps do?

_____

Have you ever been jealous of any of your friends when something good happened to them? (Circle one)   Yes   No
HOW did you behave? Were you happy? Did you tell them how great they did? Or did you put them down or talk about them behind their backs? Did you wish it were you?

Write out what you did:

_____

Daniel 6:4-5 Did these commissioners and satraps find anything wrong to accuse Daniel of?

_____

Why don't you make a list of the things you learned about Daniel in verses 3-5 in the box on the next page?

What I Learned About Daniel

Wow! Just look at Daniel! He is 80 years old, and he hasn't changed. After some people become great, they become proud. But not Daniel. These commissioners and satraps can't find anything to accuse Daniel of. First, we see there is no corruption. That means there is no bad or wicked behavior in Daniel. Remember what we learned about Daniel's character in Week One on page 32. Daniel has integrity. He is honest, trustworthy, and sincere. He does the right thing, even when no one is looking.

Now take a moment and ask yourself, "Is there anything in my life that I have done where someone could say something bad about me? Can they accuse me of telling a lie, of cheating on a test, or of stealing something?" If there is anything someone could accuse you of, write out what they could say about you.

What did you say or do?

_____

Now ask God to forgive you. Way to go!

Look at what else the commissioners and satraps say about Daniel. He is faithful. There is no negligence in him. "No negligence" means Daniel did what was required of him. He was very careful in his job. He gave it his very best!

HOW do you do your work? Your work would include chores your parents give you like cleaning the kitchen, cleaning your room, and putting away your clothes and things. It would also include your work at school.

Write out HOW you do your work. Do you do what you are asked to do? Are you careful? Do you give it your very best? Or are you sloppy and do just enough to get by? Write out WHAT you do:

_____

_____

HOW do your actions show your character? For example, you might write, "I show I try my best when I study for a test and hand in my homework."

_____

_____

_____

All right! You have done a fantastic job! Tomorrow we will find out what these commissioners and satraps do, since they can't find anything to accuse Daniel of. But before you leave the set, you need to uncover this week's memory verse.

Take a look at the awesome lions' den scene on the next page. Unscramble the words underneath the blanks in this scene to complete your verse and find out what King Darius has to say about the God of Daniel. Then look at Daniel 6 to find the reference.

"He _____ and _____ and
            eliversd   esrcues

_____ _____ and _____
    erpmfors   igsns   ondwers

in _____ and on _____, who has
      eavhen   ertha

also _____ _____ from the
     elidverde   andiel

_____ of the _____."
     owper   ilnos

Daniel 6: _____

Great work!

THE TRAP IS SET!

     Yesterday we filmed our first scene in Daniel 6 and saw that there are some very jealous commissioners and satraps. They are looking for something to accuse Daniel of so they can get rid of him. They don't want Daniel to be ruler over the entire kingdom. They want the power and prestige for themselves.

But what can they do? They can't find anything wrong in Daniel. Let's find out what happens next. Pull out your scripts and turn to page 156. Read Daniel 6:6-10 and mark the key words listed on page 112 in these verses or use your key-word bookmark.

Don't forget to mark your pronouns! And mark anything that tells you WHERE by double-underlining the WHERE in green. Mark anything that tells you WHEN by drawing a green clock 🕐 or green circle like this: ◯ .

Now roll those cameras! What are our commissioners and satraps up to?

> Daniel 6:6-7 WHAT plot do these commissioners and satraps come up with? WHAT statute and injunction (law) do they propose to the king?
>
> "Anyone who makes a _____ to any _____ or _____ besides _____, O king, for _____ days, shall be _____ into the _____ _____."
>
> Daniel 6:8 WHAT do we find out happens to this document if it is signed?
>
> _____
>
> _____

Did you know that a decree written into law by the Medes and Persians could not be changed? Why do you think this document would please King Darius? Could it be because these commissioners and satraps appeal to the king's pride? Look at how they start out in verse 6 with some praise: "King Darius, live forever!" Then there is the clincher: "If you make this statute, no one can ask anything

of any other man or god but you for 30 days." Look at how they
went straight for the king's ego: "You will be the one everyone
will come to."

Daniel 6:9 Does Darius sign this document?

_____

The trap has been set. WHAT will Daniel do?

Daniel 6:10 WHAT does Daniel do once he knows this
document is signed?

_____

_____

Daniel knows that this document means that if he prays, he
will end up in the lions' den. Is he afraid? Does he say, "I won't
pray. After all, it's only for 30 days. God will understand. He
won't want me to be thrown in the lions' den"? No. Daniel does
what?

He continued _____ on his knees. HOW many
times a day?_____

Does he hide in his room? Let's see, it says, "His
w __ __ __ __ __ s were open," which means he could
probably be seen and heard outside.

Did he whine or complain, "Why is this happening
to me"? WHAT does it say in verse 10? He gave
t __ __ __ __ s before God.

Wow! Daniel is brave. He does not fear man. Daniel is faithful to God. He knows WHO is in control of his circumstances!
Even though something bad has happened, Daniel continues to
pray just like he has always done each and every day. HOW did
Daniel pray? Daniel thanks God.

HOW about you? Do you pray every day, or do you let other things get in the way?

_____

Do you thank God even when bad things happen to you?

_____

WHAT will happen to Daniel? Darius has signed a document that cannot be changed. Will Daniel be thrown into the lions' den for praying? Don't forget to say your memory verse today!

DAY THREE

A DISTRESSED KING

"Okay—places, everyone," Aunt Sherry called out. "Are our commissioners and satraps ready? Good. Olivia, check the king's costume. All right. Now we're ready. Quiet on the set. Stand by. Roll Camera Two, Mr. Grayson. And action."

Don't forget to pray. Then turn to page 157. Read Daniel 6:11-18 and mark the key words listed on page 112 in these verses or use your key-word bookmark.

Don't forget to mark your pronouns! And mark anything that tells you WHERE by double-underlining the WHERE in green. Mark anything that tells you WHEN by drawing a green clock or green circle like this: ○.

Now come in close. Let's find out what happens to Daniel.

Daniel 6:11 WHAT do the men find Daniel doing?

_____

Daniel 6:12 WHAT did they remind the king about?

_____

Daniel 6:13 WHAT did they tell the king about Daniel?

"_____, who is one of the _____ from Judah, pays no _____ to you, or to the _____ which you signed, but keeps making his _____ three times a day."

Daniel 6:14 HOW does the king react to hearing this about Daniel?

_____

_____

Daniel 6:15 Could the king deliver Daniel? WHAT do we see about the law of the Medes and the Persians?

_____

Daniel 6:16 WHAT happens to Daniel?

_____

WHO does the king say will deliver Daniel?

_____

Daniel 6:17 WHAT was laid over the den, and HOW was it sealed?

_____

Daniel 6:18 HOW did the king spend his night?

_____

_____

_____

Just look at how the king desperately tries to find a way to save Daniel, but because of his pride in signing a document that can't be changed, there is nothing he can do. He tells Daniel, "The God you constantly serve will deliver you." Then he goes off and spends the night fasting for Daniel.

Pretty amazing that a pagan king would care about what happens to one of his captives enough to go without sleep, food, or entertainment. This shows us once again how awesome Daniel is.

WHAT will the king find in the morning? Hang in there. We'll find out tomorrow! Don't forget to practice your memory verse!

DAY FOUR

SLEEPING WITH THE LIONS

"Wow!" Max exclaimed as he and Molly walked onto the set and saw Mr. Leon, the animal trainer, working with the lions.

"Come on over," Mr. Leon called out, "and meet the lions.

We're about ready to shoot their big scene. When we're finished, I'll let you give them their treat."

Molly smiled. "They look pretty hungry to me. What if they think we're their treat?" Mr. Leon laughed. "Don't worry. I'll be right there with you."

Aunt Sherry walked up. "Everything looks good to go, Mr. Leon. I'm going to open with Camera Three on the lions, so get them ready to growl and pace around Daniel. Then we'll go to Camera Two where the camera will open wide and pan around Daniel."

"Got it," Mr. Leon answered as he snapped his whip. "Come on, fellows. We're ready for action."

Wow! Are you amazed at how huge these hungry lions are? WHAT did King Darius find the next morning after Daniel spent the night with these ferocious beasts? Let's find out.

Turn to page 158. Read Daniel 6:19-23 and mark the key words listed on page 112 in these verses or use your key-word bookmark.

Don't forget to mark your pronouns! And mark anything that tells you WHEN by drawing a green clock 🕐 or green circle like this: ◯.

Daniel 6:19 WHEN did the king rise?

_____

Did the king take his time checking on Daniel? Give King Darius his directions: Should he walk to the lions' den or run? Circle the correct answer: Walk   Run

Daniel 6:20 WHAT did Darius's voice sound like?

_____

Now give King Darius his lines. WHAT does he say to Daniel?

"Daniel, _____ of the _____ _____, has

your _____, whom you _____ _____,

been able to _____ you from the _____?"

Let's put Camera One on the opening to the lions' den. Is there any answer to King Darius's question?

Daniel 6:21 WHAT does Daniel say?

_____

Wow! Are you amazed? Not only is Daniel alive, but listen to his response: "O king, live forever!" In situations like this, a person's true character comes out. Look at the respect Daniel shows the king, who has thrown him into the lions' den. There is no anger, no bitterness, no resentment, just honor and praise.

HOW would you treat someone who had just thrown you to the lions? Think about how you would treat one of your friends if he or she hurt your feelings or betrayed you.

Would you still be nice to that person, or would you try to get even?

_____

Daniel 6:22 HOW did Daniel survive this terrible night? WHAT did God do? Draw a picture of this scene that Daniel describes in Daniel 6:22 in the box below.

HOW was Daniel found before God? (Circle one.)

Guilty   Innocent

Daniel 6:23 HOW did the king react?

He was very _____.

WHY was there no injury found on Daniel?

_____

Wow! Can someone say that about you? Can they look at your life and see that you trust God?

_____

Don't forget to practice your memory verse to remind you that God is the One who has the power to deliver and rescue.

DAY FIVE

THE KING'S NEW DECREE

"Hey, Aunt Sherry," Molly said as Sherry walked into the screening room, "we just saw the awesome footage that Mr. Grayson shot of Daniel and the lions. It is so cool! He did a fantastic job with the lions. They were so scary until the angel appeared and Mr. Leon gave them their cue."

Aunt Sherry smiled. "That's why we have Mr. Leon. Did you know that in Hollywood they call him the 'animal whisperer,' since he is so good at getting the animals to do what he wants them to do?"

"Hey, Max," Molly grinned and winked at Aunt Sherry, "maybe you should let him work with Sam."

Max petted Sam. "Don't let Molly mess with you. Just look at how good you've been." Everyone cracked up laughing.

"Okay, guys," Aunt Sherry said, "we need to get back to the set. Can you believe that this is the last scene for Season One of our television series? We need to find out what happens to those men who tricked the king into signing that document."

"Oh, man!" Max exclaimed. "That sounds like someone is in trouble to me. I can't believe this is our last day on the set. When will we get to start on Season Two?"

"It won't be long," Aunt Sherry answered. "Just as soon as everyone has a short vacation, we will start filming our next season. It will be incredible! We'll get a glimpse into the future to find out who else has visions and dreams and what they mean."

"All right," Molly said. "I can't wait!"

"Okay, guys, we need to get this season wrapped up. Molly, why don't you pray and then we can get started?"

Are you ready to film our final episode? This is going to be an awesome television series. Let's find out WHAT the king did to those men who maliciously accused Daniel. To be malicious is to want to harm someone out of spite, to have an evil motive.

Turn to page 159. Read Daniel 6:24-28 and mark the key words listed on page 112 in these verses or use your key-word bookmark.

Don't forget to mark your pronouns! And mark anything that tells you WHEN by drawing a green clock 🕐 or green circle like this: ◯.

Look at Daniel 6:24 and draw this scene that shows WHAT the king did to these men who set out to destroy Daniel. Don't forget to also show WHAT happened to their families.

Daniel 6:25 WHAT did Darius do next?

Darius the king w__ __ __ __ to all the _____,
_____, and men of every _____
who were living in all the land.

Daniel 6:26 WHAT did he make?

_____

WHAT was this decree?

_____

Wow! Look at this awesome decree! Let's make a list in the box on the next page of WHAT you learned about God in Daniel 6:22,26,27.

$\diamond$

What I Learned About God

WHAT an amazing God! Now that you know that God is the One who has the power to shut the lions' mouths, to deliver and rescue you, should you be afraid when you are in a hard and difficult situation? Will you be brave like Daniel? Will you pray and trust God, even if it means you may end up "thrown into the lions' den"?

Tell what you will do the next time something bad or scary happens to you:

_____

_____

Daniel 6:28 WHAT happened to Daniel?

_____

_____

Once again we see God's blessing on Daniel's trust and obedience to Him. Think about what Darius said in Daniel 6:20: "your God, whom you constantly serve." WHAT a testimony to be known as someone who constantly serves God. Wow! Daniel never compromises to fit into the world he lives in. Daniel fears only One, and that One is God. He is a brave man. He is willing to die to love and serve God. What a witness his life has been to these pagan kings.

As you leave the set today, ask yourself, "WHAT kind of witness am I? Do I look and act like everyone else? Or do kids and grown-ups see Jesus in my life when they look at me?"

Write out HOW you are a good witness for Jesus. Do you share Jesus with other kids? Do you turn the other cheek by not getting even if someone is mean to you? Do you help other people? Do you treat others as more important than yourself? Do you stand firm when other people try to sway you?

HOW do your actions show Jesus?

_____

_____

All right! Now say your memory verse to a grown-up. WHAT a God! Are you ready to be a Daniel? Cut and print! That was awesome. We are so proud of you!

iT'S A WRAP!

Way to go! You did it! You have helped film an amazing television series that will show people everywhere just WHO Daniel is and WHAT happens to him. Just look at all you have

learned. You know that God is a sovereign God. His name is El Elyon. He is God Most High. He is in control over all your circumstances! God is in control of EVERYTHING!

You also saw Daniel and his friends get taken into captivity. They lost their homes, their families, their language, and their names. All their hopes and dreams for their lives were changed in a moment.

Yet they never got angry or bitter. They never questioned God. Instead they made up their minds to serve God no matter what the cost. They stood firm when their faith was tested in a fiery furnace and a lions' den. They dared to be different. They were willing to give up their lives to serve the one true God. They were brave men! Are you willing to be brave like Daniel?

You also got to fast-forward into the future as God gave King Nebuchadnezzar a dream of a statue that showed four kingdoms and a stone that crushes those ten toes, the ten kings.

So far you have discovered two of those kingdoms: the kingdom of Babylon and the kingdom of the Medes and Persians. You also saw that the stone represents God's kingdom. God's kingdom will never be destroyed. It crushes all of the kingdoms and endures forever! All right!

WHO are the other two kingdoms on the statue? Just wait. You'll find out, along with some other amazing things that are going to happen in the future. You won't believe it! Wait until you see some of the cool visions and dreams. One is about four ferocious beasts. WHAT does it all mean? Find out when you join us back on the set as we film our second season on the life of Daniel: *Fast-Forward to the Future.*

Don't forget to go to www.precept.org/D4Ycertificate to print your special certificate for learning to be brave like Daniel. We are so very proud of you! Keep up the good work. See you back on the set to finish our television series on Daniel in God's Word real soon!

Molly, Max, and

(Sam)

PUZZLE ANSWERS

Page 16

"But Daniel made up his mind that he would not defile himself with the king's choice food or with the wine which he drank; so he sought permission from the commander of the officials that he might not defile himself."

Daniel 1:<u>8</u>

Page 20

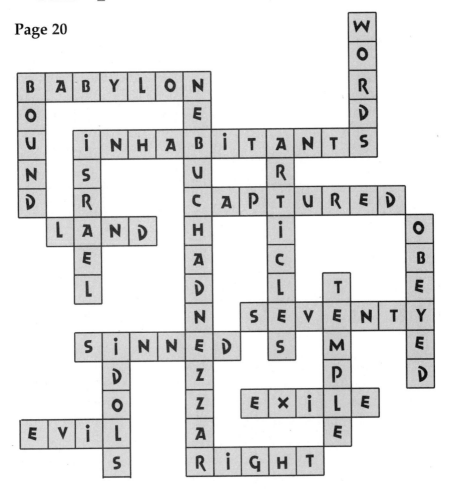

Page 42

"Daniel said, 'Let the <u>name</u> of <u>God</u> be <u>blessed</u> forever and ever, for <u>wisdom</u> and <u>power</u> belong to Him. It is He who <u>changes</u> the <u>times</u> and the <u>epochs</u>; He <u>removes</u> <u>kings</u> and <u>establishes</u> kings; He gives wisdom to <u>wise</u> men and <u>knowledge</u> to men of <u>understanding</u>.'"

Daniel 2:<u>20-21</u>

Page 49

GOLD

Nebuchadnezzar king of Babylon

SILVER

Kingdom of Medes and Persians
After Nebuchadnezzar, Inferior
Kingdom

BRONZE

Kingdom will rule over all the Earth

IRON

Strong kingdom will crush and shatter

Divided kingdom part strong, part brittle

God's Kingdom will never be destroyed. Crushes all of the kingdoms. Endures forever.

IRON & CLAY
10 KINGS

page 59

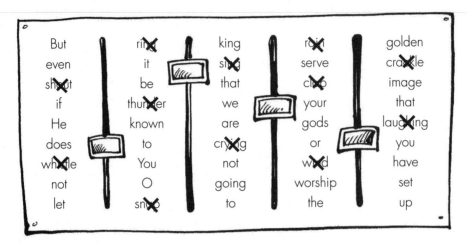

"But even if He does not, let it be known to you, O king, that we are not going to serve your gods or worship the golden image that you have set up."

Daniel 3:<u>18</u>

Page 77

"Now I, Nebuchadnezzar, <u>praise</u>, <u>exalt</u> and <u>honor</u> the <u>King</u> of <u>heaven</u>, for all His <u>works</u> are <u>true</u> and His <u>ways</u> <u>just</u>, and He is <u>able</u> to <u>humble</u> those who <u>walk</u> in <u>pride</u>."

Daniel 4:<u>37</u>

Page 85

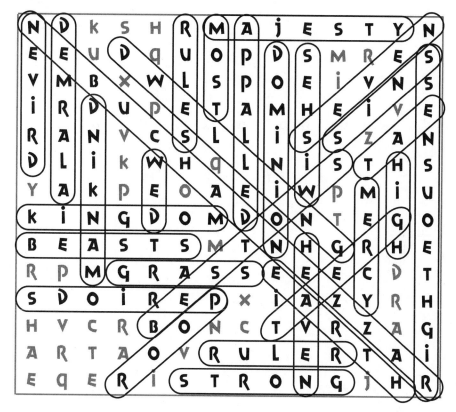

Page 98

"But the God in whose hand are your life-breath and your ways, you have not glorified."

Daniel 5:<u>23</u>

Page 116

"He <u>delivers</u> and <u>rescues</u> and <u>performs</u> <u>signs</u> and <u>wonders</u> in <u>heaven</u> and on <u>earth</u>, who has also <u>delivered</u> <u>Daniel</u> from the <u>power</u> of the <u>lions</u>."

Daniel 6:<u>27</u>

DANIEL 1-6

Chapter 1

1 In the third year of the reign of Jehoiakim king of Judah, Nebuchadnezzar king of Babylon came to Jerusalem and besieged it.

2 The Lord gave Jehoiakim king of Judah into his hand, along with some of the vessels of the house of God; and he brought them to the land of Shinar, to the house of his god, and he brought the vessels into the treasury of his god.

3 Then the king ordered Ashpenaz, the chief of his officials, to bring in some of the sons of Israel, including some of the royal family and of the nobles,

4 youths in whom was no defect, who were good-looking, showing intelligence in every branch of wisdom, endowed with understanding and discerning knowledge, and who had ability for serving in the king's court; and he ordered him to teach them the literature and language of the Chaldeans.

5 The king appointed for them a daily ration from the king's choice food and from the wine which he drank, and appointed that they should be educated three years, at the end of which they were to enter the king's personal service.

6 Now among them from the sons of Judah were Daniel, Hananiah, Mishael and Azariah.

7 Then the commander of the officials assigned new names to them; and to Daniel he assigned the name Belteshazzar, to

Hananiah Shadrach, to Mishael Meshach and to Azariah Abednego.

8 But Daniel made up his mind that he would not defile himself with the king's choice food or with the wine which he drank; so he sought permission from the commander of the officials that he might not defile himself.

9 Now God granted Daniel favor and compassion in the sight of the commander of the officials,

10 and the commander of the officials said to Daniel, "I am afraid of my lord the king, who has appointed your food and your drink; for why should he see your faces looking more haggard than the youths who are your own age? Then you would make me forfeit my head to the king."

11 But Daniel said to the overseer whom the commander of the officials had appointed over Daniel, Hananiah, Mishael and Azariah,

12 "Please test your servants for ten days, and let us be given some vegetables to eat and water to drink.

13 "Then let our appearance be observed in your presence and the appearance of the youths who are eating the king's choice food; and deal with your servants according to what you see."

14 So he listened to them in this matter and tested them for ten days.

15 At the end of ten days their appearance seemed better and they were fatter than all the youths who had been eating the king's choice food.

16 So the overseer continued to withhold their choice food and the wine they were to drink, and kept giving them vegetables.

17 As for these four youths, God gave them knowledge and intelligence in every branch of literature and wisdom; Daniel even understood all kinds of visions and dreams.

18 Then at the end of the days which the king had specified for presenting them, the commander of the officials presented them before Nebuchadnezzar.

19 The king talked with them, and out of them all not one was found like Daniel, Hananiah, Mishael and Azariah; so they entered the king's personal service.

20 As for every matter of wisdom and understanding about which the king consulted them, he found them ten times better than all the magicians and conjurers who were in all his realm.

21 And Daniel continued until the first year of Cyrus the king.

Chapter 2

1 Now in the second year of the reign of Nebuchadnezzar, Nebuchadnezzar had dreams; and his spirit was troubled and his sleep left him.

2 Then the king gave orders to call in the magicians, the conjurers, the sorcerers and the Chaldeans to tell the king his dreams. So they came in and stood before the king.

3 The king said to them, "I had a dream and my spirit is anxious to understand the dream."

4 Then the Chaldeans spoke to the king in Aramaic: " O king,

live forever! Tell the dream to your servants, and we will declare the interpretation."

5 The king replied to the Chaldeans, " The command from me is firm: if you do not make known to me the dream and its interpretation, you will be torn limb from limb and your houses will be made a rubbish heap.

6 "But if you declare the dream and its interpretation, you will receive from me gifts and a reward and great honor; therefore declare to me the dream and its interpretation."

7 They answered a second time and said, "Let the king tell the dream to his servants, and we will declare the interpretation."

8 The king replied, "I know for certain that you are bargaining for time, inasmuch as you have seen that the command from me is firm,

9 that if you do not make the dream known to me, there is only one decree for you. For you have agreed together to speak lying and corrupt words before me until the situation is changed; therefore tell me the dream, that I may know that you can declare to me its interpretation."

10 The Chaldeans answered the king and said, "There is not a man on earth who could declare the matter for the king, inasmuch as no great king or ruler has ever asked anything like this of any magician, conjurer or Chaldean.

11 "Moreover, the thing which the king demands is difficult, and there is no one else who could declare it to the king except gods, whose dwelling place is not with mortal flesh."

12 Because of this the king became indignant and very furious and gave orders to destroy all the wise men of Babylon.

13 So the decree went forth that the wise men should be slain; and they looked for Daniel and his friends to kill them.

14 Then Daniel replied with discretion and discernment to Arioch, the captain of the king's bodyguard, who had gone forth to slay the wise men of Babylon;

15 he said to Arioch, the king's commander, "For what reason is the decree from the king so urgent?" Then Arioch informed Daniel about the matter.

16 So Daniel went in and requested of the king that he would give him time, in order that he might declare the interpretation to the king.

17 Then Daniel went to his house and informed his friends, Hananiah, Mishael and Azariah, about the matter,

18 so that they might request compassion from the God of heaven concerning this mystery, so that Daniel and his friends would not be destroyed with the rest of the wise men of Babylon.

19 Then the mystery was revealed to Daniel in a night vision. Then Daniel blessed the God of heaven;

20 Daniel said,

"Let the name of God be blessed forever and ever,

For wisdom and power belong to Him.

21 "It is He who changes the times and the epochs;

He removes kings and establishes kings;

He gives wisdom to wise men

And knowledge to men of understanding.

22 "It is He who reveals the profound and hidden things;

 He knows what is in the darkness,

And the light dwells with Him.

23 "To You, O God of my fathers, I give thanks and praise,

For You have given me wisdom and power;

Even now You have made known to me what we requested of You,

For You have made known to us the king's matter."

24 Therefore, Daniel went in to Arioch, whom the king had appointed to destroy the wise men of Babylon; he went and spoke to him as follows: "Do not destroy the wise men of Babylon! Take me into the king's presence, and I will declare the interpretation to the king."

25 Then Arioch hurriedly brought Daniel into the king's presence and spoke to him as follows: "I have found a man among the exiles from Judah who can make the interpretation known to the king!"

26 The king said to Daniel, whose name was Belteshazzar, "Are you able to make known to me the dream which I have seen and its interpretation?"

27 Daniel answered before the king and said, "As for the mystery about which the king has inquired, neither wise men, conjurers, magicians nor diviners are able to declare it to the king.

28 "However, there is a God in heaven who reveals mysteries, and He has made known to King Nebuchadnezzar what

will take place in the latter days. This was your dream and the visions in your mind while on your bed.

29 "As for you, O king, while on your bed your thoughts turned to what would take place in the future; and He who reveals mysteries has made known to you what will take place.

30 "But as for me, this mystery has not been revealed to me for any wisdom residing in me more than in any other living man, but for the purpose of making the interpretation known to the king, and that you may understand the thoughts of your mind.

31 "You, O king, were looking and behold, there was a single great statue; that statue, which was large and of extraordinary splendor, was standing in front of you, and its appearance was awesome.

32 "The head of that statue was made of fine gold, its breast and its arms of silver, its belly and its thighs of bronze,

33 its legs of iron, its feet partly of iron and partly of clay.

34 "You continued looking until a stone was cut out without hands, and it struck the statue on its feet of iron and clay and crushed them.

35 "Then the iron, the clay, the bronze, the silver and the gold were crushed all at the same time and became like chaff from the summer threshing floors; and the wind carried them away so that not a trace of them was found. But the stone that struck the statue became a great mountain and filled the whole earth.

36 "This was the dream; now we will tell its interpretation before the king.

37 "You, O king, are the king of kings, to whom the God of

heaven has given the kingdom, the power, the strength and the glory;

38 and wherever the sons of men dwell, or the beasts of the field, or the birds of the sky, He has given them into your hand and has caused you to rule over them all. You are the head of gold.

39 "After you there will arise another kingdom inferior to you, then another third kingdom of bronze, which will rule over all the earth.

40 "Then there will be a fourth kingdom as strong as iron; inasmuch as iron crushes and shatters all things, so, like iron that breaks in pieces, it will crush and break all these in pieces.

41 "In that you saw the feet and toes, partly of potter's clay and partly of iron, it will be a divided kingdom; but it will have in it the toughness of iron, inasmuch as you saw the iron mixed with common clay.

42 "As the toes of the feet were partly of iron and partly of pottery, so some of the kingdom will be strong and part of it will be brittle.

43 "And in that you saw the iron mixed with common clay, they will combine with one another in the seed of men; but they will not adhere to one another, even as iron does not combine with pottery.

44 "In the days of those kings the God of heaven will set up a kingdom which will never be destroyed, and that kingdom will not be left for another people; it will crush and put an end to all these kingdoms, but it will itself endure forever.

45 "Inasmuch as you saw that a stone was cut out of the mountain without hands and that it crushed the iron, the bronze, the clay, the silver and the gold, the great God has made known to the king what will take place in the future; so the dream is true and its interpretation is trustworthy."

46 Then King Nebuchadnezzar fell on his face and did homage to Daniel, and gave orders to present to him an offering and fragrant incense.

47 The king answered Daniel and said, "Surely your God is a God of gods and a Lord of kings and a revealer of mysteries, since you have been able to reveal this mystery."

48 Then the king promoted Daniel and gave him many great gifts, and he made him ruler over the whole province of Babylon and chief prefect over all the wise men of Babylon.

49 And Daniel made request of the king, and he appointed Shadrach, Meshach and Abed-nego over the administration of the province of Babylon, while Daniel was at the king's court.

Chapter 3

1 Nebuchadnezzar the king made an image of gold, the height of which was sixty cubits and its width six cubits; he set it up on the plain of Dura in the province of Babylon.

2 Then Nebuchadnezzar the king sent word to assemble the satraps, the prefects and the governors, the counselors, the treasurers, the judges, the magistrates and all the rulers

of the provinces to come to the dedication of the image that Nebuchadnezzar the king had set up.

3 Then the satraps, the prefects and the governors, the counselors, the treasurers, the judges, the magistrates and all the rulers of the provinces were assembled for the dedication of the image that Nebuchadnezzar the king had set up; and they stood before the image that Nebuchadnezzar had set up.

4 Then the herald loudly proclaimed: "To you the command is given, O peoples, nations and men of every language,

5 that at the moment you hear the sound of the horn, flute, lyre, trigon, psaltery, bagpipe and all kinds of music, you are to fall down and worship the golden image that Nebuchadnezzar the king has set up.

6 "But whoever does not fall down and worship shall immediately be cast into the midst of a furnace of blazing fire."

7 Therefore at that time, when all the peoples heard the sound of the horn, flute, lyre, trigon, psaltery, bagpipe and all kinds of music, all the peoples, nations and men of every language fell down and worshiped the golden image that Nebuchadnezzar the king had set up.

8 For this reason at that time certain Chaldeans came forward and brought charges against the Jews.

9 They responded and said to Nebuchadnezzar the king: " O king, live forever!

10 "You, O king, have made a decree that every man who hears the sound of the horn, flute, lyre, trigon, psaltery, and bagpipe

and all kinds of music, is to fall down and worship the golden image.

11 "But whoever does not fall down and worship shall be cast into the midst of a furnace of blazing fire.

12 "There are certain Jews whom you have appointed over the administration of the province of Babylon, namely Shadrach, Meshach and Abed-nego. These men, O king, have disregarded you; they do not serve your gods or worship the golden image which you have set up."

13 Then Nebuchadnezzar in rage and anger gave orders to bring Shadrach, Meshach and Abed-nego; then these men were brought before the king.

14 Nebuchadnezzar responded and said to them, "Is it true, Shadrach, Meshach and Abed-nego, that you do not serve my gods or worship the golden image that I have set up?

15 "Now if you are ready, at the moment you hear the sound of the horn, flute, lyre, trigon, psaltery and bagpipe and all kinds of music, to fall down and worship the image that I have made, very well. But if you do not worship, you will immediately be cast into the midst of a furnace of blazing fire; and what god is there who can deliver you out of my hands?"

16 Shadrach, Meshach and Abed-nego replied to the king, "O Nebuchadnezzar, we do not need to give you an answer concerning this matter.

17 " If it be so, our God whom we serve is able to deliver us from the furnace of blazing fire; and He will deliver us out of your hand, O king.

18 " But even if He does not, let it be known to you, O king, that we are not going to serve your gods or worship the golden image that you have set up."

19 Then Nebuchadnezzar was filled with wrath, and his facial expression was altered toward Shadrach, Meshach and Abed-nego. He answered by giving orders to heat the furnace seven times more than it was usually heated.

20 He commanded certain valiant warriors who were in his army to tie up Shadrach, Meshach and Abed-nego in order to cast them into the furnace of blazing fire.

21 Then these men were tied up in their trousers, their coats, their caps and their other clothes, and were cast into the midst of the furnace of blazing fire.

22 For this reason, because the king's command was urgent and the furnace had been made extremely hot, the flame of the fire slew those men who carried up Shadrach, Meshach and Abed-nego.

23 But these three men, Shadrach, Meshach and Abed-nego, fell into the midst of the furnace of blazing fire still tied up.

24 Then Nebuchadnezzar the king was astounded and stood up in haste; he said to his high officials, "Was it not three men we cast bound into the midst of the fire?" They replied to the king, "Certainly, O king."

25 He said, "Look! I see four men loosed and walking about in the midst of the fire without harm, and the appearance of the fourth is like a son of the gods!"

26 Then Nebuchadnezzar came near to the door of the furnace

of blazing fire; he responded and said, "Shadrach, Meshach and Abed-nego, come out, you servants of the Most High God, and come here!" Then Shadrach, Meshach and Abed-nego came out of the midst of the fire.

27 The satraps, the prefects, the governors and the king's high officials gathered around and saw in regard to these men that the fire had no effect on the bodies of these men nor was the hair of their head singed, nor were their trousers damaged, nor had the smell of fire even come upon them.

28 Nebuchadnezzar responded and said, "Blessed be the God of Shadrach, Meshach and Abed-nego, who has sent His angel and delivered His servants who put their trust in Him, violating the king's command, and yielded up their bodies so as not to serve or worship any god except their own God.

29 "Therefore I make a decree that any people, nation or tongue that speaks anything offensive against the God of Shadrach, Meshach and Abed-nego shall be torn limb from limb and their houses reduced to a rubbish heap, inasmuch as there is no other god who is able to deliver in this way."

30 Then the king caused Shadrach, Meshach and Abed-nego to prosper in the province of Babylon.

Chapter 4

1 Nebuchadnezzar the king to all the peoples, nations, and men of every language that live in all the earth: "May your peace abound!

2 "It has seemed good to me to declare the signs and wonders which the Most High God has done for me.

3 "How great are His signs
And how mighty are His wonders!
His kingdom is an everlasting kingdom
And His dominion is from generation to generation.

4 "I, Nebuchadnezzar, was at ease in my house and flourishing in my palace.

5 "I saw a dream and it made me fearful; and these fantasies as I lay on my bed and the visions in my mind kept alarming me.

6 "So I gave orders to bring into my presence all the wise men of Babylon, that they might make known to me the interpretation of the dream.

7 "Then the magicians, the conjurers, the Chaldeans and the diviners came in and I related the dream to them, but they could not make its interpretation known to me.

8 "But finally Daniel came in before me, whose name is Belteshazzar according to the name of my god, and in whom is a spirit of the holy gods; and I related the dream to him, saying,

9 'O Belteshazzar, chief of the magicians, since I know that a spirit of the holy gods is in you and no mystery baffles you, tell me the visions of my dream which I have seen, along with its interpretation.

10 'Now these were the visions in my mind as I lay on my bed: I was looking, and behold, there was a tree in the midst of the earth and its height was great.

11 'The tree grew large and became strong

And its height reached to the sky,

And it was visible to the end of the whole earth.

12 'Its foliage was beautiful and its fruit abundant,

And in it was food for all.

The beasts of the field found shade under it,

And the birds of the sky dwelt in its branches,

And all living creatures fed themselves from it.

13 'I was looking in the visions in my mind as I lay on my bed, and behold, an angelic watcher, a holy one, descended from heaven.

14 'He shouted out and spoke as follows:

" Chop down the tree and cut off its branches,

Strip off its foliage and scatter its fruit;

Let the beasts flee from under it

And the birds from its branches.

15 "Yet leave the stump with its roots in the ground,

But with a band of iron and bronze around it

In the new grass of the field;

And let him be drenched with the dew of heaven,

And let him share with the beasts in the grass

of the earth.

16 "Let his mind be changed from that of a man

And let a beast's mind be given to him,

And let seven periods of time pass over him.

17 "This sentence is by the decree of the angelic watchers

And the decision is a command of the holy ones,

In order that the living may know

That the Most High is ruler over the realm of mankind,

And bestows it on whom He wishes

And sets over it the lowliest of men."

18 'This is the dream which I, King Nebuchadnezzar, have seen. Now you, Belteshazzar, tell me its interpretation, inasmuch as none of the wise men of my kingdom is able to make known to me the interpretation; but you are able, for a spirit of the holy gods is in you.'

19 "Then Daniel, whose name is Belteshazzar, was appalled for a while as his thoughts alarmed him. The king responded and said, 'Belteshazzar, do not let the dream or its interpretation alarm you.' Belteshazzar replied, ' My lord, if only the dream applied to those who hate you and its interpretation to your adversaries!

20 'The tree that you saw, which became large and grew strong, whose height reached to the sky and was visible to all the earth 21 and whose foliage was beautiful and its fruit abundant, and in which was food for all, under which the beasts of the field dwelt and in whose branches the birds of the sky lodged—

22 it is you, O king; for you have become great and grown strong, and your majesty has become great and reached to the sky and your dominion to the end of the earth.

23 'In that the king saw an angelic watcher, a holy one, descending from heaven and saying, "Chop down the tree and destroy it; yet leave the stump with its roots in the ground, but with a band of iron and bronze around it in the new grass of the field, and let him be drenched with the dew of heaven, and let him

share with the beasts of the field until seven periods of time pass over him,"

24 this is the interpretation, O king, and this is the decree of the Most High, which has come upon my lord the king:

25 that you be driven away from mankind and your dwelling place be with the beasts of the field, and you be given grass to eat like cattle and be drenched with the dew of heaven; and seven periods of time will pass over you, until you recognize that the Most High is ruler over the realm of mankind and bestows it on whomever He wishes.

26 'And in that it was commanded to leave the stump with the roots of the tree, your kingdom will be assured to you after you recognize that it is Heaven that rules.

27 'Therefore, O king, may my advice be pleasing to you: break away now from your sins by doing righteousness and from your iniquities by showing mercy to the poor, in case there may be a prolonging of your prosperity.'

28 "All this happened to Nebuchadnezzar the king.

29 " Twelve months later he was walking on the roof of the royal palace of Babylon.

30 "The king reflected and said, 'Is this not Babylon the great, which I myself have built as a royal residence by the might of my power and for the glory of my majesty?'

31 "While the word was in the king's mouth, a voice came from heaven, saying, 'King Nebuchadnezzar, to you it is declared: sovereignty has been removed from you,

32 and you will be driven away from mankind, and your dwell-

ing place will be with the beasts of the field. You will be given grass to eat like cattle, and seven periods of time will pass over you until you recognize that the Most High is ruler over the realm of mankind and bestows it on whomever He wishes.'

33 "Immediately the word concerning Nebuchadnezzar was fulfilled; and he was driven away from mankind and began eating grass like cattle, and his body was drenched with the dew of heaven until his hair had grown like eagles' feathers and his nails like birds' claws.

34 "But at the end of that period, I, Nebuchadnezzar, raised my eyes toward heaven and my reason returned to me, and I blessed the Most High and praised and honored Him who lives forever;

For His dominion is an everlasting dominion,

And His kingdom endures from generation to generation.

35 "All the inhabitants of the earth are accounted as nothing,

But He does according to His will in the host of heaven

And among the inhabitants of earth;

And no one can ward off His hand

Or say to Him, 'What have You done?'

36 "At that time my reason returned to me. And my majesty and splendor were restored to me for the glory of my kingdom, and my counselors and my nobles began seeking me out; so I was reestablished in my sovereignty, and surpassing greatness was added to me.

37 "Now I, Nebuchadnezzar, praise, exalt and honor the King of heaven, for all His works are true and His ways just, and He is able to humble those who walk in pride."

Chapter 5

1 Belshazzar the king held a great feast for a thousand of his nobles, and he was drinking wine in the presence of the thousand.

2 When Belshazzar tasted the wine, he gave orders to bring the gold and silver vessels which Nebuchadnezzar his father had taken out of the temple which was in Jerusalem, so that the king and his nobles, his wives and his concubines might drink from them.

3 Then they brought the gold vessels that had been taken out of the temple, the house of God which was in Jerusalem; and the king and his nobles, his wives and his concubines drank from them.

4 They drank the wine and praised the gods of gold and silver, of bronze, iron, wood and stone.

5 Suddenly the fingers of a man's hand emerged and began writing opposite the lampstand on the plaster of the wall of the king's palace, and the king saw the back of the hand that did the writing.

6 Then the king's face grew pale and his thoughts alarmed him, and his hip joints went slack and his knees began knocking together.

7 The king called aloud to bring in the conjurers, the Chaldeans and the diviners. The king spoke and said to the wise men of Babylon, "Any man who can read this inscription and explain its interpretation to me shall be clothed with purple and have

a necklace of gold around his neck, and have authority as third ruler in the kingdom."

8 Then all the king's wise men came in, but they could not read the inscription or make known its interpretation to the king.

9 Then King Belshazzar was greatly alarmed, his face grew even paler, and his nobles were perplexed.

10 The queen entered the banquet hall because of the words of the king and his nobles; the queen spoke and said, "O king, live forever! Do not let your thoughts alarm you or your face be pale.

11 "There is a man in your kingdom in whom is a spirit of the holy gods; and in the days of your father, illumination, insight and wisdom like the wisdom of the gods were found in him. And King Nebuchadnezzar, your father, your father the king, appointed him chief of the magicians, conjurers, Chaldeans and diviners.

12 "This was because an extraordinary spirit, knowledge and insight, interpretation of dreams, explanation of enigmas and solving of difficult problems were found in this Daniel, whom the king named Belteshazzar. Let Daniel now be summoned and he will declare the interpretation."

13 Then Daniel was brought in before the king. The king spoke and said to Daniel, "Are you that Daniel who is one of the exiles from Judah, whom my father the king brought from Judah?

14 "Now I have heard about you that a spirit of the gods is in you, and that illumination, insight and extraordinary wisdom have been found in you.

15 "Just now the wise men and the conjurers were brought in before me that they might read this inscription and make its

interpretation known to me, but they could not declare the interpretation of the message.

16 "But I personally have heard about you, that you are able to
give interpretations and solve difficult problems. Now if you are
able to read the inscription and make its interpretation known to
me, you will be clothed with purple and wear a necklace of gold
around your neck, and you will have authority as the third ruler
in the kingdom."

17 Then Daniel answered and said before the king, " Keep your
gifts for yourself or give your rewards to someone else; however,
I will read the inscription to the king and make the interpretation known to him.

18 "O king, the Most High God granted sovereignty, grandeur,
glory and majesty to Nebuchadnezzar your father.

19 "Because of the grandeur which He bestowed on him, all the
peoples, nations and men of every language feared and trembled
before him; whomever he wished he killed and whomever he
wished he spared alive; and whomever he wished he elevated
and whomever he wished he humbled.

20 "But when his heart was lifted up and his spirit became so
proud that he behaved arrogantly, he was deposed from his
royal throne and his glory was taken away from him.

21 "He was also driven away from mankind, and his heart was
made like that of beasts, and his dwelling place was with the
wild donkeys. He was given grass to eat like cattle, and his body
was drenched with the dew of heaven until he recognized that

the Most High God is ruler over the realm of mankind and that He sets over it whomever He wishes.

22 "Yet you, his son, Belshazzar, have not humbled your heart, even though you knew all this,

23 but you have exalted yourself against the Lord of heaven; and they have brought the vessels of His house before you, and you and your nobles, your wives and your concubines have been drinking wine from them; and you have praised the gods of silver and gold, of bronze, iron, wood and stone, which do not see, hear or understand. But the God in whose hand are your life-breath and your ways, you have not glorified.

24 "Then the hand was sent from Him and this inscription was written out.

25 "Now this is the inscription that was written out: 'MENĒ, MENĒ, TEKĒL, UPHARSIN.'

26 "This is the interpretation of the message: 'MENĒ'—God has numbered your kingdom and put an end to it.

27 "'TEKĒL'—you have been weighed on the scales and found deficient.

28 "'PERĒS'—your kingdom has been divided and given over to the Medes and Persians."

29 Then Belshazzar gave orders, and they clothed Daniel with purple and put a necklace of gold around his neck, and issued a proclamation concerning him that he now had authority as the third ruler in the kingdom.

30 That same night Belshazzar the Chaldean king was slain.

31 So Darius the Mede received the kingdom at about the age of sixty-two.

Chapter 6

1 It seemed good to Darius to appoint 120 satraps over the kingdom, that they would be in charge of the whole kingdom,

2 and over them three commissioners (of whom Daniel was one), that these satraps might be accountable to them, and that the king might not suffer loss.

3 Then this Daniel began distinguishing himself among the commissioners and satraps because he possessed an extraordinary spirit, and the king planned to appoint him over the entire kingdom.

4 Then the commissioners and satraps began trying to find a ground of accusation against Daniel in regard to government affairs; but they could find no ground of accusation or evidence of corruption, inasmuch as he was faithful, and no negligence or corruption was to be found in him.

5 Then these men said, "We will not find any ground of accusation against this Daniel unless we find it against him with regard to the law of his God."

6 Then these commissioners and satraps came by agreement to the king and spoke to him as follows: "King Darius, live forever!

7 "All the commissioners of the kingdom, the prefects and the satraps, the high officials and the governors have consulted together that the king should establish a statute and enforce an

injunction that anyone who makes a petition to any god or man besides you, O king, for thirty days, shall be cast into the lions' den.

8 "Now, O king, establish the injunction and sign the document so that it may not be changed, according to the law of the Medes and Persians, which may not be revoked."

9 Therefore King Darius signed the document, that is, the injunction.

10 Now when Daniel knew that the document was signed, he entered his house (now in his roof chamber he had windows open toward Jerusalem); and he continued kneeling on his knees three times a day, praying and giving thanks before his God, as he had been doing previously.

11 Then these men came by agreement and found Daniel making petition and supplication before his God.

12 Then they approached and spoke before the king about the king's injunction, "Did you not sign an injunction that any man who makes a petition to any god or man besides you, O king, for thirty days, is to be cast into the lions' den?" The king replied, "The statement is true, according to the law of the Medes and Persians, which may not be revoked."

13 Then they answered and spoke before the king, "Daniel, who is one of the exiles from Judah, pays no attention to you, O king, or to the injunction which you signed, but keeps making his petition three times a day."

14 Then, as soon as the king heard this statement, he was deeply

distressed and set his mind on delivering Daniel; and even until sunset he kept exerting himself to rescue him.

15 Then these men came by agreement to the king and said to the king, "Recognize, O king, that it is a law of the Medes and Persians that no injunction or statute which the king establishes may be changed."

16 Then the king gave orders, and Daniel was brought in and cast into the lions' den. The king spoke and said to Daniel, "Your God whom you constantly serve will Himself deliver you."

17 A stone was brought and laid over the mouth of the den; and the king sealed it with his own signet ring and with the signet rings of his nobles, so that nothing would be changed in regard to Daniel.

18 Then the king went off to his palace and spent the night fasting, and no entertainment was brought before him; and his sleep fled from him.

19 Then the king arose at dawn, at the break of day, and went in haste to the lions' den.

20 When he had come near the den to Daniel, he cried out with a troubled voice. The king spoke and said to Daniel, "Daniel, servant of the living God, has your God, whom you constantly serve, been able to deliver you from the lions?"

21 Then Daniel spoke to the king, "O king, live forever!

22 "My God sent His angel and shut the lions' mouths and they have not harmed me, inasmuch as I was found innocent before Him; and also toward you, O king, I have committed no crime."

23 Then the king was very pleased and gave orders for Daniel

to be taken up out of the den. So Daniel was taken up out of the den and no injury whatever was found on him, because he had trusted in his God.

24 The king then gave orders, and they brought those men who had maliciously accused Daniel, and they cast them, their children and their wives into the lions' den; and they had not reached the bottom of the den before the lions overpowered them and crushed all their bones.

25 Then Darius the king wrote to all the peoples, nations and men of every language who were living in all the land: "May your peace abound!

26 " I make a decree that in all the dominion of my kingdom men are to fear and tremble before the God of Daniel;
For He is the living God and enduring forever,
And His kingdom is one which will not be destroyed,
And His dominion will be forever.

27 "He delivers and rescues and performs signs and wonders
In heaven and on earth,
Who has also delivered Daniel from the power of the lions."

28 So this Daniel enjoyed success in the reign of Darius and in the reign of Cyrus the Persian.

INDUCTIVE BIBLE STUDIES
DISCOVER 4 YOURSELF®
FOR KIDS!

BRING THE WHOLE COUNSEL OF GOD'S WORD TO KIDS!

▼ GENESIS

God's Amazing Creation (Genesis 1–2)
Digging Up the Past (Genesis 3–11)
Abraham, God's Brave Explorer (Genesis 11–25)
Extreme Adventures with God (Genesis 24–36)
Joseph, God's Superhero (Genesis 37–50)

◀ 2 TIMOTHY

Becoming God's Champion

◀ JAMES

Boy, Have I Got Problems!

ESTHER ▶

God Has Big Plans for You, Esther

◀ REVELATION

Bible Prophecy for Kids (Revelation 1–7)
A Sneak Peek into the Future (Revelation 8–22)

DANIEL ▶

You're a Brave Man, Daniel! (Daniel 1–6)
Fast-Forward to the Future (Daniel 7–12)

▲ TOPICAL & SKILLS

God, What's Your Name? (Names of God)
Lord, Teach Me to Pray (for Kids)
How to Study Your Bible (for Kids)
  also available in DVD
Cracking the Covenant Code (for Kids)

JONAH ▶

Wrong Way, Jonah!

◀ GOSPEL OF JOHN

Jesus in the Spotlight (John 1–10)
Jesus—Awesome Power, Awesome Love (John 11–16)
Jesus—To Eternity and Beyond (John 17–21)